FOSTERING INVENTIVENESS IN CHILDREN

Sheila J. Henderson

and

Rosemarie K. Moore

ISBN: 1453798749
ISBN 13: 9781453798744

Library of Congress Control Number: 2013902768
CreateSpace Independent Publishing Platform
North Charleston, South Carolina

Why is inventing so much fun?

Acknowledgments

Gratitude goes first to our husbands for reading our drafts and cooking the many dinners while we worked on this book and to our families who had confidence in our endeavor. We are also grateful to our editors who gave us enthusiastic guidance throughout the book's development, and to those generous individuals who reviewed our drafts and provided their frank wisdom: Rickson Sun—Chief Technologist at IDEO, Lydia Bird—author of *Sonnet: One Woman's Voyage from Maryland to Greece*, Mihalyi Cszikszentmihalyi—author of *Flow* and *Creativity*, Ken Goodman—author of *In Defense of Good Teaching and Saving our Schools*, Nancy Fitzgerald—poet and author of *An Inward Facing Out*, Gwendolyn Wooddell—Professor and former school teacher, Craig Forte, LCSW—Private practice and consulting in Palo Alto, California, Joanne Dzegilenko—School teacher also in Palo Alto, Raja Jasti—Engineering consultant in Cupertino, California, Indira Narayanswamy, Sushila Venkatraman, Keith and Tracey Wycoff—Planet Biotechnology in Fremont, California, and Meg Hardin at Alliant International University in San Francisco. Finally, we would also like to express gratitude to the inspiration from the Silicon Valley inventors who inspired this book, and from Professors Anthony L. Antonio, Robert Roeser, and John D. Krumboltz—all from Stanford University. To all of you, we thank you.

Dedication

To Krishna, and

To Charley, and

To Rosemarie and Charley's children
Jeffrey, Kimberly, and Laurel, and

grandchildren Hannah, Nicholas, Andres, and Carlos

Table of Contents

Authors' note

Children are creative in their every day lives in a manner that often goes unnoticed by adults. It shows up as *natural talent* because most very young children have had no formal training in creativity yet still exhibit originality in their thinking and behavior. They are also naturally inventive. This book is about fostering this inventiveness in children!

If you have opened up this book, you are probably interested in engaging children in new and different activities—those that interest you as well. You are likely to be a pioneer in your interests in fostering inventiveness in children, and we want to support you in this process of bringing new and exciting learning opportunities to children. We anticipate that you, like so many people interested in doing novel things, are likely to be busy with nary a minute for researching an invention curriculum. For this reason, the sequel to this book, *Invention Friday Curriculum*, offers a step-by-step young inventors' lesson plan, so you can get started with fostering inventiveness in children in your chosen environment.

In a website publication on the Young Inventors Program entitled, *"Meant to Invent! Teacher Guide,"*[1] the American Academy of Sciences explained that inventing is an activity that gives children critical choices in which they can engage their multiple intelligences at home, in the community, and in schools. By fostering inventiveness in children, parents, teachers, and community participants will be taking one positive step in preparing children now to approach problems with courage and curiosity and inventiveness, within their own unique intelligences.

The ability to solve real world problems with invention is critical for our new generations of young people. They will be looking for new approaches to issues that have surpassed our greatest minds to date, such as global warming, climate change, and others. If we encourage new generations of young inventors, the Academy of Applied Science argued, then invention and innovation could continue to produce the kind of transformative achievements that were accomplished in the 19th and 20th centuries.

The central question in our book is: *How can parents, educators, and administrators collaborate together to foster an inventive spirit in children, such that they are inspired to pursue a lifetime of positive and rewarding achievement?*

Our book addresses this question by offering stories about young inventors, demonstrating that kids can invent. We talk about the psychology that underlies creativity and invention, and present inventing as an interaction between emotion, thought, and action, with clear examples. We suggest the key to inventing is creating an environment conducive to inventive learning and suggest ways for parents and teachers to do just that. For young school children and pre-adolescents, we talk about some of the best young inventor programs around the country, and offer games, book and Internet resources through which children and adults can learn about invention.

In the sequel to this book, *Invention Friday Curriculum*, the flexible lesson plans are designed as weekly 1-2 hour young inventor trainings through a 9-month school year—an "Invention Friday" series of lesson plans, inspired by the National Public Radio tradition of "Science Friday."[2] Consistent with California education standards, we also offer tools for ongoing evaluation of students' progress relative to the "Invention Friday" weekly learning objectives and the students' social, emotional, and cognitive development. Our hope is that these lesson plans will make it a little easier for a parent or volunteer to bring an "Invention Friday" program to a school, either in the classroom or after school. The plans are also ideal for home schooling. Then for the younger toddlers at home or in preschool, we offer resources for parents or preschool teachers to prepare the youngest children for later, more formal "Invention Friday" training.

Keep in mind that a young inventors program does not have to be an expensive endeavor. One method to accomplish a young inventors program *without* investing a lot of cash is to ask the families of students to pool their leftover and/or scrap resources for supplies. Other than the loan of a computer with Internet access, a digital camera, glue guns, scissors, and some light tools like pliers. Most of the other supplies needed for "Invention Friday" are old glue sticks, rubber bands, paper, tape, odds and ends like paper towel rolls, old hardware (screws, nails), jar lids, flimsy old forks and spoons, cardboard, and used egg cartons!

In closing, we applaud your commitment to children and hope you will enjoy the process of fostering their inventiveness. By all accounts, inventing is fun, and children love it! Enjoyment is the essential key. The key to helping students to acquire skills in inventing is to provide the training in a forum that is flexible, enjoyable, and allows for a high level of personal creative expression.

Let's prepare our children to tackle the toughest of world problems!

2013 Sheila J. Henderson and Rosemarie K. Moore

www.inventionfriday.org

(All links in paper copies of this book are available for easy clicking on our website)

CHAPTER I

What does it mean to be an inventor?

The stereotype

When the movie, *Back to the Future*, hit the theaters, Hollywood created one more eccentric image of an inventor. "Doc Brown" or "Doc," was the wild-eyed, reclusive, and energetic inventor with mussed hair, crumpled clothes, who modified a DeLorean car to travel back and forth in time. The dilemma with this image is that while "Doc Brown" was indeed clever, the character may not have been a parent's first choice of career role model for their children.

The media image of the eccentric inventors, like "Doc Brown," hardly typifies today's inventor, quite the opposite. In order to foster the *inventive spirit* in children, perhaps the first step is to foster a more realistic image of the inventors who have shaped our world. The truth is that today's inventors may be thinking in wild dimension, but they are unlikely to look as outlandish as "Doc Brown." Humble and behind the scenes, many inventors are real people who simply focus their energies on creating useful products, processes, and ideas.

The irony is that the inventors of the products that define our daily lives are hardly remembered. Who invented the toaster, the cup holder, and contact lens? The great legends of Ben Franklin, Thomas Edison, Henry Ford, and Marie Curie are taught in school, but what about all the others?[3] Take for example, the inventor of the first refrigerated truck in 1949. Frederick McKinley Jones,[4] apparently orphaned at eight years old, was a self-taught African-American man who lived his life with a *spirit of inventiveness*. He was a World War I veteran, who responded to the problem of food spoiling on trucks driven over long distances. He figured out a way to put refrigeration in trucks and revolutionized the transportation of food. After that accomplishment, Frederick McKinley just kept on inventing, solving problem after problem, and eventually earning 60 patents to his name. Not many people may know about Frederick McKinley, but his story could very well inspire a child to listen to his or her own ideas, dare to develop them, and see these ideas come to life.

The real story about inventors and invention

Who are inventors?

Many people think of inventors as individuals who create new and distinctive products, such as Dean Kamen[5] and the *Segway*. See Figure 1. Others may think of inventors as professional designers at firms, such as IDEO headquartered in Palo Alto, California, who create solutions for customers (e.g., the ultimate utility bike[6]). Others might know engineers and scientists who work in incubators, such as The Foundry[7], or large development labs within corporations, such as Xerox, Hewlett Packard, and IBM. These professionals create astonishing inventions. The examples above, however, are not the only type of inventors who create remarkable solutions.

Figure 1: The Personal Transporter (PT) ® was designed by Dean Kamen as a novel human transporter with a self-balancing technology for forward and backward maneuvering, emissions free, powered by rechargeable NiMH battery packs. Permission to use photo courtesy of Segway Inc.®

Neurobiologists, for example, who are usually thought of as scientists, can be thought of as *scientist-inventors* who toil for long days and nights in labs, seeking to discover vital new processes. Take brain cell regeneration as an example—such a discovery could change lives of people all over the globe. Another example of a type of professional who impacts our world is a social architect. Edward Zigler,[8] a social architect-inventor who master-minded Project Head Start, started a social innovation program for low-income families. These examples illustrate that the term *inventors*, in the broadest sense, can include individuals who apply their creative talents in ways that improve our ability to thrive.

Most recently, inventive individuals have created new scientific processes (gene splicing), developed tools that lead to other inventions (new software programming languages), and/or applied new methods to old concepts (solar heating). Others have invented new approaches to music, literature, fine art, photography, and illustration (Bob Dylan, Wallace Stegner, Jackson Pollock, Ansel Adams, and Dr. Seuss), new ways of depicting the news (political satire cartoonists), new social opportunity (micro credit loans in Bangladesh), and new views on lifestyle choices (organic foods, green products). From one second to the next, those who may not be commonly identified as inventors are actively changing our daily lives.

The original question posed was: *Who are inventors?* Perhaps a more penetrating question is: *When does a creative idea actually become an "invention" per se?*

The nature of invention

The variety of terms used to characterize an invention may distract from an accurate understanding of the creativity and market potential of an invention. Terms such as, "create," "innovate," "develop," "design," "discover," "improve," and "disrupt" are used along side or in place of the term "invent." This proliferation of terms perhaps reflects the struggle within the English language to capture the nuance and variety of human endeavor that inspire an invention.

The crux of the issue may be that while some inventions leapfrog existing technology (e.g., the light bulb vs. candle lantern), most inventions improve on existing technology (e.g., Amoxicillin vs. penicillin). Innovation in its purest definition may more accurately refer to technology improvements, yet it is pervasively used in technology circles to characterize products that verifiably alter technology. For simplicity, the term *invention* is used exclusively throughout this book, even though the term itself can be controversial. For example, Hewlett Packard Company once embraced *HP-Invent* as a corporate branding campaign. IDEO, on the other hand, avoids the term "inventor" in their corporate identity preferring the term "designer" as more apropos to their culture.[9]

One broad definition of invention is as follows: *An invention is created through the production of novel ideas, processes, or products that solve a problem, fit a situation, or accomplish a goal in a way that is novel, implementable, useful, cost-effective, and alters, or otherwise said, disrupts an aspect of technology, accepted process, or current state of knowledge.*[10]

In the above definition, five 'musts' of true invention emerge: (a) novelty, (b) implementability, (c) utility, (d) cost-effectiveness, and (e) disruptive to existing technology. To illustrate how these five criteria might apply to an invention, the terms are compared with a Rube Goldberg illustration below of an invention to wash storefront windows. Though creative and humorous, does this mechanical window washing contraption qualify as a true invention?

How To Keep Shop Windows Clean   RUBE GOLDBERG (tm) RGI 031

Figure 2: Rube Goldberg's window washing invention: "Rube Goldberg stands in front of an x-ray and sees an idea inside his head showing how to keep shop windows clean. Passing man (A) slips on banana peel (B) causing him to fall on rake (C). As handle of rake rises it throws horseshoe (D) onto rope (E) which sags, thereby tilting sprinkling can (F). Water (G) saturates mop (H). Pickle terrier (I) thinks it is raining, gets up to run into house and upsets sign (J) throwing it against non-tipping cigar ash receiver (K) which causes it to swing back and forth and swish the mop against window pane, wiping it clean." Permission to use: Rube Goldberg is the (R) and (c) of Rube Goldberg Inc.

Here, we put Rube Goldberg's window washing assembly to the test against the terms: *novel, implementable, useful, cost-effective,* and *disruptive*. When compared to existing technology for window washing (hand-washing), a Rube Goldberg's window-washing design—a mechanical window washer—would be something new to see. *Novelty* distinguishes an invention from what exists today. However to fit the definition posed above, Rube Goldberg's invention has to satisfy more criteria.

The practicality of this invention poses a problem. Goldberg's window washing machine could possibly qualify as an invention due to its low *cost*, and it may even pass as *useful* and *disruptive* to the usual process of washing store windows by hand. However, what about the *implementability* and *cost-effectiveness* of this invention? Looking again at the cartoon, one can see that the movement of the mechanical window washer depends on the happenstance event of a passerby stepping on the banana peel, slipping, and falling on the rake. This uncertainty, plus the additional drawback of endangering potential customers, would lead most raters to fail the Goldberg contraption on *implementability* and *effectiveness*. Thus, Rube Goldberg's machine remains as a memorable parody on invention.

Spotting an inventor

Inventors are people who likely approach the world from a unique perspective. Like many artists, inventors may have a different lens through which they experience each day. A fine artist might be fascinated with form, texture, color and natural light. An inventor is someone who is likely to notice what about life is simply inefficient and needs a better solution. An inventor observes what things work well enough but could be improved. In contrast to the media image sometimes portrayed, inventors are more likely to be noticed for their approach to the world around them, than for their eccentricity. The design firm IDEO, mentioned earlier, and the Stanford University Design program call this *design thinking*[11]—a certain way of approaching the world.

Annoyance can be the creative spark

Many people adapt quickly to certain inconveniences in life, whereas an inventor may become visibly disconcerted by less than perfect circumstances. In a 1994 book chapter[12] entitled, "Creativity and its Discontents," Professor Mark Runco at University of Georgia made a convincing argument that annoyance can be a tremendous spark for creative action. Consider how many of us take annoyances in stride, such as maneuvering a clumsy ironing board or spending the nth hour on folding those awkward fitted sheets. An inventor, however, may become particularly annoyed or intrigued and begin to ponder ways to solve the inefficiency.[13]

Friends, co-workers, and spouses might look askance while inventors complain persistently about the inconvenience of having to walk outside to get the daily paper, or the frustration caused by shoelaces that won't stay tied. Similarly, parents may feel as if they just cannot bear one more "why" question from their child. The "complainer" may just be the one who is *thinking* and *feeling* like an inventor, just as an "exhaustingly inquisitive child" may actually have the *curiosity* of an inventor.

Creative kindling for inventors

Just as kindling is essential to building a fire, it takes more than one creative spark to accomplish an invention. Moving from a creative spark to actual invention takes character—personal qualities[14] that the San Jose Tech Museum of Innovation in San Jose, California terms *invention kindling* (e.g., curiosity, attitude, focus, persistence, drive, passion, a playful spirit, and more). In inventors, it is the sense of annoyance at inefficiency and unwillingness to accept the status quo mentioned above, which sparks the creative energy that in turn puts creative kindling into play.

■ curiosity ■ determination ■ faith ■ tenacity ■ nerve ■ creativity
■ fun ■ timing ■ vision ■ commitment ■ confidence
■ communication ■ trust ■ synergy ■ freedom ■ acceptance ■

Figure 3: Personal qualities known as "kindling" to successful invention as shown in a 2003 wall exhibit at the San Jose Tech Museum of Innovation in San Jose, California.

Expert problem-finders

A related characteristic of inventors is their orientation toward *problem-finding*[15] (also noted in artists[16]). When "complaining" about an inconvenience, an inventor may actually be engaging in problem-finding. Though accidents and unexpected events have inspired some inventions[17] (e.g., silly putty, post-it notes, the pacemaker, and the microwave), most inventions are deliberate solutions to problems in the current state of technology. The process of inventing new products involves problem-finding (i.e., identifying unmet needs and zeroing in on the underlying technological and social conundrums) and then *solution-finding* new ideas. Inventors therefore can be thought of as expert problem- and solution-finders in their individual fields of discovery.

Problem-finding is so central to the process of inventing, that some design programs teach the art of problem-finding (such as the Stanford Product Design Program, now called the Stanford Design Program). To teach problem-finding, instructors[18] may encourage their graduate students to create a list of problems in daily life, such as the annoyance of losing keys, feeling drowsy when driving, and so forth. This list of problems is called a *"bug" list.*[19] Once their "bug" lists are created, students may then be asked to solve a small set of the problems through prototyping,[20] which is a method of sketching, modeling, and or building by trial and error. Problem-finding and "bug" lists can also be integral to the innovation process of success-ful inventors. Because children have the fresh, hands-on experience with their world, as they learn to navigate the inconveniences of the adult world, we argue that young inventors may be naturally suited for this process of problem-finding.[21]

The story of how Tom Blanchard[22] invented the apple-paring machine is a good example of a young person using the problem-finding process. In 1801 Tom wanted to do something important. He apparently had a seri-ous speech impediment, and in those days (often still now[23]), there was little tolerance in the classroom for Tom's stutter. After being thrown out of school, one can imagine that Tom may have been trying to restore his sense of worth by inventing something exceptionally novel for the annual apple harvest contest. Tom may not have been able to recite poetry in class, but it appears that he had the *courage to invent.*

Every year during the apple harvest, teams would compete to be the fastest apple peelers in the town. Tom wanted to win the competition, but because he had not yet identified the core problem associated with rap-id apple peeling, his team had no particular advantage. Wrestling with this conundrum, Tom apparently remembered hearing about an apple-paring machine in Boston. In no time, Tom realized that human hands could only pare so fast. Gambling that a machine could leap frog the current "by hand" process, Tom sketched, designed, and built different approaches to paring apples mechanically. The core problem was the difficulty in replicating the dexterity of the human thumb. Eventually after trial and error (or "proto-typing"[24] as mentioned above), he invented a dexterous machine that peeled apples so fast, no human team could match the speed of his invention. Tom met his need to out-peel his competition by developing something that was *novel, implementable, cost-effective, useful*, and *completely disrupted* the locally accepted process of hand-peeling large quantities of apples.

Inventors over history

How have inventors changed over the century?

In the early 1900s, Joseph Rossman surveyed inventors who had patents registered with the government. In publications dated 1935 and 1964, Rossman reported that inventors of his time were young when they made their first invention (average age was 21 years old). Twenty respondents made their first invention from 5 to 9 years old. Most inventors (75%) had been awarded their first patent between ages 15 to 35.

A closer look at this early 20th century data reveals that the major-ity (64%) of the inventor respondents had four or more patents, averaging 46 patents each. That fact poses the question: *Do all inventors hold patents?* Consider Charles Richard Drew, MD (1904-1950),[25] an American medical doctor interested in finding a way to transport blood to soldiers in World War II. In his distinguished doctoral thesis entitled, "Banked Blood: A Study in Blood Preservation," Dr. Drew researched alternatives for blood pres-ervation. Though he may never have received a patent, Dr. Charles Drew succeeded in inventing the life-saving process for storing blood. He was later named the first African American Director of the Red Cross Blood Bank. This is one clear example of how an unpatented invention not only saved countless lives in World War II but also *altered* the landscape of emergency medicine.

Similar to number of patents, *less education did not necessarily mean less impact* in the 20th century. Consider what inventor Frederick McKinley Jones (1892-1961) mentioned earlier was able to accomplish with only eight years of formal education. Without a high school or college education, Frederick McKinley Jones made it possible to transport perishable food over long distances—a *lifestyle-altering* invention.

Since Rossman's time, technology has advanced exponentially as has the technical complexity of inventing work. In this respect, the demand for technically agile and creative minds has spurred the availability of higher education in math, sciences, and engineering. In a more recent 2002 study[26] of 247 people making a living by inventing, the inventors were older (19-74), more highly educated (68% of the respondents had graduate degrees), and potentially more experienced (averaging 14 years of inventing experience). In a larger European study of roughly 8,900 inventors,[27] the average age and level of education of these inventors appeared commensurate with the smaller 2002 U.S. study. Back in the early 1990's, apparently all of Rossman's respondents were European American men. Roughly a century later, among those who responded to the U.S. inventor survey, there was one women for every four men (23%) making a living by inventing, and one person of color for every five (20%) European-American inventors. In the studies on inventors in Canada,[28] in Australia,[29] and in Europe,[30] the ratios of women to men were much less favorable.

Women and people of color as inventors

What is an example of the enduring *inventive spirit* in women? On a day of particularly miserable weather around 1905, Mary Anderson[31] hopped on a streetcar. She apparently vowed to help when observing a driver, white-knuckled, trying to navigate snow and sleet sticking to his front car window. Not long after, Mary Anderson was awarded a U.S. Patent for her sketches of window wipers.

These stories of early pioneering women can be inspiring for children, especially young girls. Consider Dr. Ellen Ochoa.[32] She was the first Latina female to become an astronaut in 1990. In addition to her interstellar accomplishments, she was also an inventor. Dr. Ochoa created three patented inventions in the optical aerospace technology area (e.g. optical inspection systems). In the late 1800s, Judy W. Reed[33] did not let her educational disadvantage stop her *inventive spirit*. Ms. Reed, a creative African-American woman, may not have known how to read, but in 1884 she was awarded a patent for a machine she developed to knead and roll dough. In 1885 Sarah Goode,[34] also African American, received a patent for her design of a "cabinet bed" (see Figure 4). Now more than a century later, "Murphy beds," are sold as space-saving options around the world. Both Ms. Reed and Ms. Goode were the first African American women to receive patents.

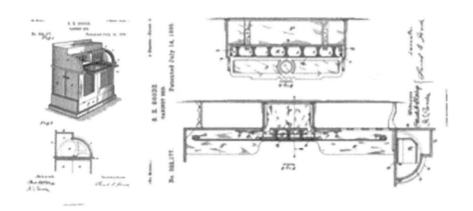

Figure 4: Drawings from Sarah E. Goode's Cabinet Bed patented July 14, 1885 patent # 0322177

Even though European American inventors may have held the center stage in corporate America and in history books, African-, Asian-, Latino-, and Native American inventors have been steadily making an impact on U.S. culture and technology since the early 1800s and prior. The high proportion of European American male inventors by no means diminishes the actual impact of women and people from underrepresented cultural groups in the inventing world. Despite the well-known limits upon social, political, educational, and economic opportunity to people of color and to women over history, ethnic and cultural minorities too have transformed the world we live in. Consider the inventions by diverse and native Americans and immigrants to this country: carbon filament in the light bulb (Lewis Latimer),[35] peanut butter (George Washington Carver), first manufactured yo-yo (Pedro Flores), optical diagnostic equipment (Tuan Vo-Dinh), carbon dioxide laser (Kumar Patel), abacus (indigenous culture), Lacrosse (Native American)—these are but a few. Diverse peoples continue to contribute prolifically to the current technological/cultural revolution. Because opportunities for technical contribution are opening up around the world and due to the Internet's unprecedented capacity for global communication, one can now hope for a fuller participation of diverse peoples in invention.

Conclusion

With a notable simplicity and complexity, parsimony and efficiency, effectiveness and elegance, inventors from diverse backgrounds, cultures, and belief systems have solved problems in novel ways for centuries. Inventors have worked alone, in pairs, or as a team with or without social, economic, and educational privilege to come up with original and effective solutions to problems. Inventions created by people of all walks of life endure because they are affordable, valuable and useful to society. Ironically, the spark of invention may begin with frustration over minor inconveniences, and an unwillingness to accept the status quo. Then with admirable character, inventors seize this tension with a keen *inventive spirit* and continue to transform our world.

The stories about inventors and their experiences tell us that inventing takes energy, curiosity, enthusiasm, trust in one's own abilities, perseverance, drive, tenacity, and willingness to risk failure. Thomas Alva Edison[36] is often quoted: "Genius is one percent inspiration, and ninety-nine percent perspiration." [37] Apparently this famous inventor of the incandescent lamp made 10,000 prototyping attempts before honing in on the perfect design for the light bulb. Studies have also shown, just what is commonly observed, that the invention process is challenging, fraught with setbacks, but also deeply enjoyable and rewarding to the creator. For many invention teams, it turns out that humor, playfulness and fun is vital to the creative process.

Further reading for children

On invention:

Frederick McKinley Jones (1893-1961). (1996-2008). *Black history pages.* Retrieved from: http://www.blackhistorypages.net/pages/fjones.php

Jones, C. F. (1998). *Accidents may happen: Fifty inventions discovered by mistake.* NY: Delacorte Press.

Jones, C. F. (1991). *Mistakes that worked: 40 Familiar inventions and How they came to be.* NY: Delacorte Press.

Ott, M. V. and Swanson, G. M. (1994). *I've got an idea! The story of Frederick McKinley Jones.* Minneapolis, MN: Runestone Press.

Roberts, R. M. (1989). *Serendipity: Accidental discoveries in science.* NY: John Wiley & Sons.

Royston, M. & Roberts, J. (1994). *Lucky science: Accidental discoveries from gravity to velcro, with experiments.* NY: John Wiley & Sons.

Thimmesh, C. (2000). *Girls think of everything: Stories of ingenious inventions by women.* Boston: Houghton Mifflin.

Tucker, T. and Loehle, R. (1995). *Brainstorm! The stories of twenty American kid inventors.* NY: Farrar Straus & Giroux.

Further reading and resources for adults

On invention and design:

Brown, T. (2008, June). Design thinking. *Harvard Business Review.*

For more publications by Tim Brown at IDEO, see: http://www.ideo.com/people/tim-brown

Brown, T. with Littman, J. (2001). *The art of innovation: Lessons in creativity from IDEO, America's leading design firm.* NY: Doubleday.

MacFarquhar, L. (1999, December 6). Looking for trouble: How an inventor gets his best ideas. *The New Yorker,* 78-93.

Welcome to the virtual crash course in design thinking. (2013). Stanford University Institute of Design, retrieved at: http://dschool.stanford.edu/dgift/

Wolfe, M. F. (2000). *Rube Goldberg: Inventions.* NY: Simon & Schuster.

On women inventors:

Borges, P. (2007). *Women Empowered: Inspiring change in the emerging world.* NY: Rizzoli.

United States Patent and Trademark Office. (1990). *Buttons to biotech (1996 update report with supplemental data through 1998): Patenting by women, 1977 to 1988. Update is available at:* http://www.uspto.gov/web/offices/ac/ido/oeip/taf/wom_98.pdf

On Sheila Henderson's (1st author) inventor studies:

Henderson, S. J. (2004a). Product inventors and creativity: The finer dimensions of enjoyment. *Creativity Research Journal, 16*(2 & 3), 103-126.

Henderson, S. J. (2004b). Inventors: The ordinary genius next door. In R.J. Sternberg, E. L. Grigorenko and J. L. Singer (Eds.), *Creativity: From potential to realization* (pp. 293-312). Washington DC: American Psychological Association.

Henderson, S. J. (2002). Correlates of inventor motivation, creativity, and achievement. Doctoral dissertation, Stanford University. *Dissertation Abstracts International.*

Sheila Henderson's publications are available at: http://www.researchgate.net/profile/Sheila_Henderson/publications/

CHAPTER 2

Who says children are too young to invent?

The concept of "kid inventors" is not a new one;[38] over the last century, children have held patents. Though the US Patent and Trademark Office does not collect information on the age of patent holders,[39] there are plenty of stories in library books and on the Internet about children who have been successful at inventing.[40] One good example of a young inventor is Sydney Dittman, four years old at the time of her invention, who was awarded a patent in 1993 for a tool to grasp round knobs.[41] See Figure 5.

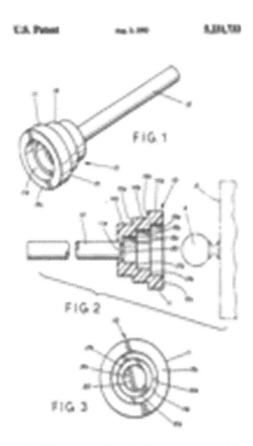

Figure 5: August 3, 1993 patent sketch illustrating a tool for grasping round knobs by Sidney Dittman, who began inventing at four years old (patent #5,231,733 and #D344,662).

Jacob Dunnack,[42] is an example of a young child who followed his inventive spirit but may not have pursued a patent. At six years old during a car trip, Jacob looked forward to playing ball when he and his family arrived at his grandmother's house. Finally there, Jacob and his father prepared to go outside to play ball, then realized that his mother had remembered his bat but not his balls. What disappointment!

Weeks later back in school, Jacob was asked to create a project for the Connecticut Invention Convention (described below) at his school. Without hesitation, Jacob knew just what he wanted to do. With the help of his parents, Jacob carved out one of his wooden bats just enough to store several balls and sealed the bat with a Styrofoam cork (see figure 6). This way wherever he took his bat, along went the baseballs. This new idea was apparently a fabulous success at the convention for young inventors. Jacob went on to sell his invention in a large toy store. Of course Jacob is a lot older now, but his six-year old invention story is inspiring for many children whose parents and teachers recognize their inventive spirit.

These stories suggest that children can and have been successful inventors, so perhaps it is a matter of providing more opportunities for children to invent so they can rise to their full inventive potential.

Figure 6: Jacob Dunnack and his batball invention. With permission to reproduce from Elizabeth Dunnack, Jacob's mother. Courtesy of Willimantic Camera & Video

Children, inventiveness, and art

Many of those who teach and lead teams of inventors discuss the idea of elegance in invention—that aesthetic appeal may also be as important as the five "musts" of an invention discussed in Chapter I. As we consider, children's potential as inventors, this combination of an invention's practicality and aesthetic appeal raises one important question. Do children have natural potential in art?

Just as there is evidence that children can invent, there is evidence that children have natural potential in art. There are contemporary examples of children producing globally recognized artwork. One example is Wang Yani[43] born in Southern China in 1975, who started painting at 3 years old, probably best known for her brush technique in animating baboons. Ms. Yani has received international recognition as the youngest artist to have a solo show at the Smithsonian Museum in Washington D.C. Many other children artists, who aren't yet famous have also demonstrated their talent. One example is Alex Bismuth, the young artist in Figure 7. In the photo, this young artist's works—created at age five (left) and age ten (right)—were being sold in someone's backyard during an Open Studios art event in Palo Alto, California, during which his mother, Fabienne Bismuth, was also featuring her artwork.

Figure 7: Alex Bismuth and his art creations. Permission to use photo granted by Alex and Fabienne Bismuth.

In 1967, Nelson Goodman founded Project Zero in the School of Education at Harvard University, which afforded some of the most influential research in creativity at the time. Researchers there noticed that there was similarity in the expressive quality between the work of professional artists and the artwork of children. According to the results from Project Zero's research, when the art of young children was judged according to aesthetic criteria used to judge the work of adult artists, such as symbolic representation, balance, variation in use of line, children held their own.[44]

"It is preschool children's drawings that are most often thought to contain the expressive quality of work of adult artists," explained Jessica Hoffman Davis[45] who was the founding Director of the Arts in Education program at Harvard University's School of Education. Unfortunately though as Davis goes on to say, "Between ages eight and 11, what Project Zero researchers described as the 'flavorfulness' of children's drawings, is on the decline." In her 2008 book entitled, *Why Our Schools Need the Arts,* Davis in turn explained how children's involvement with the arts in school can give them the opportunity to continue to grow artistically and also serve as a foundation for learning in other disciplines, including the sciences.

Often when children enter school and are given the traditional realism art assignments, they will struggle with the representational tasks. Children can get discouraged when they see their drawings are different from what they see, and label themselves as "bad drawers." As a result of their discouragement, many may not pursue their artistic potential.

John Ruggieri,[46] founder of Abstraction Made Elementary (AME) worked for nearly ten years with pre-adolescent children teaching abstract art in Boston, Massachusetts. Ruggieri's approach was unique. He encouraged children to create their experience of the world around them not in the way it "should look like" but in the way that they experienced a particular element of the world. In this way, AME circumvented putting children through the discouragement of representational tasks. As a reporter for *Newsweek* wrote:[47] "A veteran of the program, Willis T. Burke, [at that time, 11 years old]... says he has to follow the rules in other classes; a dragon must look like a certain kind of dragon. The visiting artists teach youngsters to loosen up." Figure 8 displays one of Willis T. Burke's paintings, among several abstracts by children featured in a public exhibition of AME student artwork at the Harvard Graduate School of Education. His painting was also featured on the exhibition invitation postcard. "AME is all about process," Ruggieri explained. "I try to teach kids that abstract art is incredibly fluid, that it's about using the visible world to make something truly inventive and unusual, but that it can involve representational art, too. I would rather have them bring something to a work that they like than push for total abstraction; I mean, if they want to bring Tweety in, that's fine."[48] AME also found ways to include digital learning by loosening the bounds of what could be included in their images.

The students were challenged to question whether representational art is superior to abstract depictions of what they see and experience in the world.

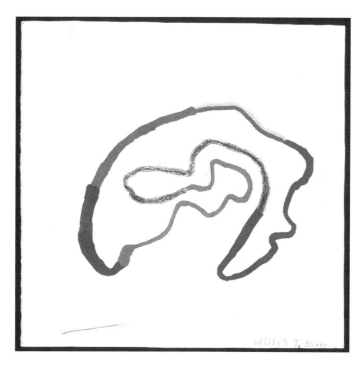

Figure 8: Painting by Willis T. Burke, created at age eight. Permission to use photo granted by John Ruggieri © 1998-2001 Abstraction Made Elementary. Photo courtesy Susan Byrne Photography. All Rights Reserved.

Elliot Eisner, now Emeritus Professor with the School of Education at Stanford University, taught a graduate course called *Artistic development of the child*. Eisner who has written extensively on the topic, presented a passionate and convincing argument that young children develop artistic talent as part of their normal human development. Eisner asserts that they can continue their artistic development given optimal environmental circumstances and with appropriate instruction. The availability of such opportunities, however, is sometimes hard to come by in schools under financial stress.

Nature versus nurture

Are children born with inventive *and* artistic spirits? Can children become inventors and designers without parental encouragement and school programs? In the aforementioned 2002 study of 247 inventors,[49] the inventor participants were asked through an online survey to write about their childhood experiences with inventing. The resulting stories suggested for most of the participants, their inventive and creative spirits emerged early in life. Even though specifically asked about school experiences and adult encouragement, some inventors remembered their inventive spirits as innate. *"I never needed encouragement,"* one inventor shared, *"I've been doing this since I was 3, according to my parents."* Another however specifically wrote about the encouragement of parents:

> *Together with my dad, we "invented" and built a new musical instrument that I named the Pedong. It had a pedal that let you vary the tension on a rubber band that you plucked. It wasn't a great invention, but I *felt* like an inventor. This was formative when I was young. I kept the image.*

... or, some noted the concern their parents had about what might happen next.:

> *Inventing is fun - it's an adult term for what kids do all the time. If anything I'd say I was discouraged from inventing as a child - after I shorted out the house electrics, my (non-technical) parents were somewhat worried by some of my activities!"*

One inventor submitted a story about how he problem-solved to avoid the dreaded naptime:

> *I was always taking things apart since before I could remember. My mother told me a story...as a baby I snuck a screwdriver into my crib for a nap. I proceeded to take the crib apart while I was in it. The crib crashed all around me and I slid out the bottom. Since my mother didn't know how to put it back together I didn't have to take my nap. Whenever I would look at something I would always analyze it mentally wondering how it was built and how I could change it or fix it to meet my needs better. I still do this constantly. It's instinctual.*

23

Clearly, the vignette stories generated in this study (similar to above) will not settle the longstanding *nature versus nurture* debate. The vignettes provide anecdotal evidence however that, whether through active encouragement or through parents tactfully looking the other way, most participants acknowledged the presence of their inventive and creative spirits early in life.

Fantasy and imagination in childhood

Spontaneous imagination and fantasy come to children naturally. According to Yale Emeritus Professor and author, Jerome Singer, imagination and fantasy are considered critical to the healthy development of children.[50] Stories about how children use imagination as a way to solve problems in their world are abundant. In her 2001 book, *Imaginary Companions and the Children Who Create Them,* Marjorie Taylor, a Professor of Psychology at Oregon State University psychologist discussed imaginary friends as a normal, creative form of play, through which children can create elaborate entertainment but also work through solutions to many of their personal concerns. For example, creative children from 2 -12 years old may invent imaginary friends to communicate emotions that they may not be ready to take responsibility for (i.e., "Lolly is angry that you said that"), to cover for mistakes for which they fear repercussions (i.e., "Jack did it, not me"), or among many other things, to express fear or anxiety (i.e., "Marcy is not dressed yet, so we better not leave yet for school").

The New Yorker magazine once featured an article (September 20th, 2000), "Bumping into Mr. Ravioli," where writer Adam Gopnik told a story about his own daughter's imaginary friend. His daughter Olivia had invented a friend, Charlie Ravioli. Unlike Andrea and her imaginary pet alligator who were constant companions during times of loneliness, Charlie Ravioli never had time for Olivia. Observing this, her concerned father soon caught on that his daughter's imaginary friend was a revealing allegory. Olivia was growing up in a world of overextended adults who often did not have time for her. Writer and father Gupnik had listened carefully to Olivia's conversations with Charlie Ravioli. Often Charlie would reply to Olivia, "I'm busy right now, perhaps later," just as many adults often said in Olivia's real life.

When is active imagination useful for adults?

Case Western Reserve Professor of psychology, Sandra Russ, referred to the fantasy process in child's play in her 1993 book, *Affect and Creativity*, as a blending of thoughts, feelings, and mental images often occurring in imagination, fantasy, and in daydreams. These processes also appear critical to the inventive process of adult writers, inventors, and other creative people. David Levy, a popular inventor who was featured in the December 6, 1999 issue of *The New Yorker* magazine, talked about relying on, for his inventing success, a "fantasy method" while lying in bed.

Sheila Henderson's (author) interview study with inventors[51] found evidence that this imagination and fantasy process was an integral part of the invention process, where some adult inventors appeared to similarly blend their thoughts, feelings, and mental images to do their daily work. Two of the inventors recounted how motivating imagination could be. As one inventor participant neared the point of discovery, he said he would imagine the public fanfare his invention would receive:

> "I get extremely emotional, like [a] puppy wags its tail. I'm thinking of a dozen doctors who I want to show this to."

Another way this same inventor described the usefulness of fantasy was:

> "Sometimes you just kind of like float away, in the mind, so deep. It's just a matter of how much you can insulate yourself from anything else around. And then as deeper you can go into that, somehow you just go and picking up those ideas ... Just a matter of finding yourself and understanding yourself, how to get there."

If adults can keep alive their natural childhood talents of imagination and fantasy, this ability may foster discovery work.

What is available for training our young inventors?

Several programs deserve mention as examples of how adults are supporting the inventive spirit in children. In 2007, the US Patent and Trade Office (USPTO) joined forces with the National Inventors Hall of Fame's *InventNow* (www.invent.org) to promote a national "Inspiring Invention" campaign to put an engine behind the USPTO's traditionally underfunded efforts to support inventiveness in children. As a result, three out of the four invention programs offered by the National Inventors Hall of Fame's *InventNow* support children:

1. *Camp Invention* is a national program that brings invention to K-6 children in schools, by way of a one-week summer program offering one of four modules (i.e., *Discover, Create, Spark,* and *Geo-Quest*), each offering unique programs so that Camp Invention can be repeated the next year with a new module to the same children.

2. *Club Invention* offers support and activities for after school invention activities for grades 1-6. Club invention offers six modules entitled, *Bolder Builders*™, *Castles, Catapults, and Coats of Arms*™, *E.Z. Science*™, *Flight Sight* ™, *Passage to Planet ROG*™, *Phys. Ed: Physics in Motion, SOS: Endangered Earth*™, and *Trash Island: A Garbage Patch Journey*™.

3. *Inspiring Invention* directs website visitors to www.inventnow.org, which is an interactive, online environment where children, 8-11 years, can do research about inventions, experiment with their own inventions, and register them once developed.

Through these programs, *InventNow* is fostering inventiveness in children by promoting the idea young people can and do invent, and backing up that idea with learning resources.

Apart from *InventNow,* the USPTO also offers schoolteachers, *i-CREATM,* which is a series of free online curricula for teaching invention in elementary, middle, and high schools (www.uspto.gov/kids/kids-tm-curriculum.jsp). In addition, there are organizations around the country that are making a difference by bringing children opportunities to invent. Two of these programs—the Connecticut Invention Convention (CIC) and the Young Inventors' Program®—collaborate with school systems around the country to promote young inventor programs.

The Connecticut Invention Convention (CIC) (http://www.ctinventionconvention.org/) is a nonprofit organization that encourages young inventors in Connecticut schools and holds an annual competition for K-8 participants. In their annual convention, hundreds of young inventor finalists go to a convention center to present their inventions. One can hear the buzz of excitement as the many corporate sponsored awards are given out for various novelties in the inventions. See Figure 9.

Figure 9: An aerial view of a Connecticut Invention Convention where young inventor finalists are displaying their inventions. Photo included with permission from the CIC.

The Academy of Applied Science (AAS) offers a Young Inventors' Program® (http://www.aas-world.org/YIP/index.html) for schools in New Hampshire, Nevada, New York and Massachusetts. The AAS Young Inventors Program® provides teacher guides (*Meant to Invent!®*) and support free teacher workshops to introduce K-8 children to critical thinking and important problem solving skills through invention. AAS also offers the opportunity for students to bring their inventions to an Annual Celebration.

There have been other entrepreneurial resources available to children, such as an online game called *Hot Shot Business*—a project developed for children interested in learning how to start a business, co-sponsored by Disney and the Kauffman Foundation; unfortunately, this game has been discontinued. In Menlo Park, California, there is an organization called *BUILD* (http://www.build.org/), which is a non-profit organization offering in school training on entrepreneurship to young people in 9th grade and after school entrepreneurship training for young people in grades 10-12. Here is one student's experience (printed with permission from the BUILD website):

> *My freshman year I joined BUILD, an organization for young*
> *entrepreneurs in under-developed communities like East Palo*
> *Alto. In BUILD I learned all aspects of business and wrote a*

30-page business plan that I presented in front of 300 people at Stanford Business School. My team's business plan won first place. I glowed with confidence.

As stated on their website, "BUILD is a youth entrepreneurship and college-preparation program that uniquely works with students at highest risk of dropping out of high school. Founded with four students in East Palo Alto in 1999, BUILD now works with 700 students annually and operates five sites nationwide."

Because of these programs and others,[52] the question is no longer, *Can young people invent?* It is now, *What can adults do at home, in the community, and in the educational system to foster this natural inventive spirit in young people?*

Sometimes one person will have the skills to be both an inventor *and* an entrepreneur. Far more often, however, an inventor will team up with an entrepreneur in a start up venture to bring a product, process, or idea to the market. A successful economy will have ample inventors who have access to entrepreneurs, with whom they can form productive partnerships. Many graduate business schools around the country now offer formal training in entrepreneurship. The same applies to graduate invention training. Formal university-based training in engineering is offered in undergraduate and graduate programs throughout the country. Several programs are most noted for their invention and design training, such as the Massachusetts Institute of Technology, Stanford University Hasso Plattner Institute of Design (D-School), and the Hasso Plattner Institute in Berlin, Germany

Why wait until college to begin inventor training?

Many young children may need direction, belief in themselves, and inspiration to pursue the math and science curriculum in middle school. High school students must show a promising level of proficiency in math and science to be accepted into most colleges. If a child's interest for inventing is engaged in preschool through 5th grade, then that excitement about inventing may build enthusiasm for math and science. Then, this interest in elementary school math and science may make the middle school and high school courses more accessible. The hope is that these same young people would then pursue the math, science, and other challenging courses in college that are becoming critical to many 21st century professions.

Other options for inspiring young inventors are the many good books written to encourage young inventors. A few of the "must have" books are listed below under *Further reading*. Sometimes local public libraries are willing to purchase requested books or will find them for city or county residents through interlibrary loan systems.

If book resources, curricula, and inventor programs are available, why then have schools been slow to adopt young inventor programs as part of their curricula? Often private after-school programs for inventors will exist for a few years then die out. These programs require community collaboration between funding organizations, parents, teachers, and schools. Some programs, however, have been able to sustain themselves for a decade or more. With the right support an idea for a young inventors' clubhouse in someone's backyard could blossom into a program that benefits hundreds of children over decades.

Conclusion

It is clear that children develop inventive spirits and artistic talent quite naturally. Kids use emotion, intellect, fantasy, and imagination to solve problems. Over a lifetime, adults gather knowledge and intuition. The unique thing that children have is a fresh perspective and an affinity for having fun. Fostering this childhood sense of inventiveness and creativity, however, is critical to having future adult inventors needed to further our human progress, to surmount the problems of the 21st century, and to establish peaceful co-existence.

Invention games for children and adults

Outset Media (2007). *Professor Nuggin's famous inventions card game.* Victoria, BC, Canada. For ages 3 and above: 2-8 players.

Pazow! Corporation (2005). *The invention game.* For ages 12 and above: 3 or more players.

Invention at Play (No date). Invention Playhouse. Lemelson Center for the Study of Invention and Innovation. http://inventionatplay.org/playhouse_main.html

Further reading for children

On young artists and inventors:

Egan, L. H. (1997). *Inventors and inventions.* NY: Scholastic Professional Books.

Erlbach, A. (1997). *The kids' invention book.* Minneapolis, MN: Lerner Publishing Group.

Harper, C. M. (2001). *Imaginative inventions: The who, what, where, when, and why of roller skates, potato chips, marbles, and pie and more!* London, England: Little, Brown, & Co.

Wuffson, D. L. (1997). *The kid who invented the popsicle and other inspiring stories about inventions.* NY: Cobblehill Books.

Zhensun, Z. and Low, A. (1991). *A young painter: The life and paintings of Wang Yani—China's extraordinary young artist.* NY: Scholastic.

Further reading for adults

On invention:

Flatow, I. (1993). *They all laughed . . . from light bulbs to lasers: The fascinating stories behind the great inventions that have changed our lives.* NY: Harper Collins.

Hérbert, T. P., Karnes, F. A., & Stephens, K. R. (2005). *Inventions and inventing for gifted students.* Austin, TX: Prufrock Press.

Invention: Enhancing inventiveness for quality of life, competitiveness, and sustainability. (2004). Report of the Committee for Study of Invention. Retrieved from: http://web.mit.edu/invent/report.html

Weber, R. J. (1992). *Forks, phonographs, and hot air balloons: A field guide to inventive thinking.* NY: Oxford University Press.

On children's natural talent in art:

Camhi, L. (2006, June 18th). If a little genius lives in the house, what's on the fridge?" *The New York Times,* Art Section, p. 34.

Davis, J. H. (2008). *Why our schools need the arts.* NY: Teachers College Press.

Kindler, A. M. (1997). *Child development in art.* Reston, VA: National Art Education Association

On the nature versus nurture debate:

Sapolsky, R. M. (2004). *Why zebras don't get ulcers.* NY: Owl Books. In this book, Dr. Robert Sapolsky emphasized that the general debate of nature versus nurture is not necessarily an "either or" issue but more likely one of the gene "expression" that occurs as people experience different environmental influences.

Simonton, D. (1999). *Origins of genius: Darwinian perspectives on creativity.* NY: Oxford University Press.

Sternberg, R. J. (Ed.). (1999). *Handbook of creativity.* NY: Cambridge University Press.

CHAPTER 3:

Support, play, and differences in enjoyment and learning

There are strategies for creating optimal environments at home and in school for toddlers and young children that can make a big difference in fostering inventive and creative potential.

Support and play

At home in the earliest years when creativity first emerges, the more parents foster a life space that provides psychological and physical safety and acceptance of their children's development, the more their children's creativity is likely to flourish. As Case Western Reserve Professor of Psychology Sandra Russ explained, the early years are when, "play and imagination, a predictable living environment, openness to ...[emotional] expression, and ...[emotional] investment in the child by the parents"[53] can make a tremendous difference.

Longitudinal studies, those that follow the same individuals over time, can offer convincing evidence about the critical dimensions of a home environment in fostering creative behavior. There is a particularly good 1987 longitudinal study conducted by a psychology professor at University of California at Santa Cruz, David Harrington and colleagues. In their 1987 paper, Harrington et al.[54] explained that by following 106 families with preschool children, they examined the patterns between specific parents' child-rearing practices and children's scores on creativity potential scales over time through childhood and early adolescence. They found a significant positive correlation between a supportive parenting style and the creativity potential of those children in early adolescence. Important examples of the child rearing practices that were associated with later creative potential were: (a) respect for children's opinions, (b) time for daydreaming, thinking, and loafing, (c) offering choices to enhance child decision-making and autonomy, (d) encouragement of curiosity, exploration, and questioning, (e) appreciation and acknowledgement of a child's effort towards accomplishing tasks, and last but certainly not least, (f) warmth and intimacy in the home.

Scholars have also studied the impact of expressive play on child development and the ways in which adults can encourage it in their children's daily lives.[55] Emeritus Professor Jerome Singer and Senior Research Scientist Emeritus Dorothy Singer at Yale University have been prominent and influential in state-of-the-art understanding of imagination and play in the development of creative behavior. Together, the Singers have authored a number of useful books for ways that adults can encourage imagination and play in children.[56] For example in their 2001 paperback, *Make-Believe: Games and Activities for Imaginative Play,* the Singers recommend parent participation in imaginative play with children at home. Make believe games, according to the Singers, give children opportunities to express themselves and to try out role behaviors that they observe in the world around them. Through imagination in play, a child may talk and act with unseen animals, engage in pretend play with imagined people, and may even reach out to bring other children or adults in their imaginative world.

For the child who plays alone with imaginary figures and objects, a parent can join in and encourage the child's expressive play.[57] The Singers recommend encouragement of children's imaginative play by both teachers and parents, by offering adequate space and materials, old clothes for costume, and even the suggestion of themes by taking "play" roles themselves. Just as reading aloud to children invites visual participation with the characters and scenes in the mind's eye, adults playing "as if" are encouraging openness in imaginative self-expression.

Our greatest caution in discussing this topic is: *Guard your child's time for imaginative play*. "Academic training is increasingly replacing imaginative play and experiential hands-on learning in the early years of our children's lives," reminds the Alliance for Childhood.[58] In their Fact Sheet on *Healthy Play*,[59] the Alliance for Childhood makes five recommendations to parents: (a) reduce or eliminate TV screen time, (b) plan time for self-initiated play, (c) choose simple toys, such as boxes, blocks, sand, clay, and dolls that lead children to creating their own imaginative play, (d) encourage outdoor adventure, and (e) bring back the art of hands-on work (cooking, raking, or washing the car). These five actions are influential in inspiring play and exploration.

There is evidence to suggest that social changes all over the world are presenting barriers to open playtime for children. In a study across 16 nations, the Singers interviewed mothers in countries of Europe, Africa, Asia, and North and South America and asked them to rate how their own children spent their time each day. The results were similar across continents: The major activity noted for their children was watching television. Free play and experiential learning activities were apparently mentioned far less frequently.

Television is an obvious contrast to free play, because most TV requires little, if any,[60] of the active engagement crucial to a child's physical, behavioral, emotional, and cognitive development. Some selective uses of television, however, can be useful to child development.[61] Some television programs, electronic and computer games, and online learning options—if well supervised—do have potential to offer excellent learning opportunities. See *Further reading* below for more on this topic.

The United Nations High Commission for Human Rights has declared *play* is a human right of every child,[62] because free play is so critical to the optimal development of children. The American Academy of Pediatrics explained the process of play as follows:[63]

Play allows children to use their creativity while developing their imagination, dexterity, and physical, cognitive, and emotional strength. Play is important to healthy brain development. It is through play that children at a very early age engage and interact in the world around them. Play allows children to create and explore a world they can master, conquering their fears while practicing adult roles, sometimes in conjunction with other children or adult caregivers. As they master their world, play helps children develop new competencies that lead to enhanced confidence and the resiliency they will need to face future challenges. Undirected play allows children to learn how to work in groups, to share, to negotiate, to resolve conflicts, and to learn self-advocacy skills. When play is allowed to be child driven, children practice decision-making skills, move at their own pace, discover their own areas of interest, and ultimately engage fully in the passions they wish to pursue.

The Strong National Museum of Play in New York, also a good source on play, is dedicated to providing a space where families engage in different forms of play. This Museum also endorses play as critical to learning and human development.

Many social forces in addition to television compete with free play. Families that can afford after school activities now make choices among an array of sports, dance, music, art, and other activities—each family grappling with how much is too much in terms of over-scheduling children; some families cannot afford many after school activities, if any, and may find that electronic choices compete with their children's play environments. Many inner city neighborhoods lack safe areas for children to gather and engage in outside free play at all, making boys and girls clubs critical to opportunities for spontaneous play gatherings. When both parents carry full-time employment and long commute times between work and home, time for family play can be scarce.

After-school programs during the K-5 school years can offer a peer environment for social experiences, homework help, sports, and areas of open play for exploratory or creative activities. In this potential open play environment, children construct pretend activities together, use many words, phrases and feelings in expression of their roles, bring about a broader vo-cabulary and emotional awareness through their very engaged play together. Free time and unstructured playtime can also give time to experiment with social roles and group organization, as children establish roles and rules of play in spontaneous games. Group play allows for conflict negotiation and rapid creative resolutions so the fun can continue. These are all forms of skill development that are critical to later adult life.

Differences in enjoyment and learning

In his two books, *Flow: The psychology of Optimal Experience* and *Creativity: Flow and the Psychology of Discovery and Invention*, Mihalyi Csikszentmihalyi explained that the process of active and deep involvement in an activity can be at the heart of creative behavior. By observing how, when, and in what situations children actively focus and apply themselves, teachers and parents can gather important clues to what their children enjoy doing and in what situations they are most likely to learn effectively. What activities tend to inspire the most active engagement? What activities seem to invite only passive interest? Board games, class projects, recess play, sports involvement, reading, and collaborative activities can powerfully stimulate a child's development. Each child however will tend to engage differently in these activities—one child may look forward to come home from school to read a book, whereas another child may prefer to play at the local park.

Individual differences in learning appear early in elementary education, and some of these are gender based and culturally extended.[64] Hormonal differences beginning in gestation continue into childhood and adolescence with influence on the rate and direction of brain development. Some leading neurologists who study brain development and function in children with the latest technology agree that there are differences in brain function between girls and boys, but caution on the extent of the differences.[65]

Girls and boys seem to excel in school at different ages.[66] Boys can have difficulty as they enter formal education at ages five, six, or seven; whereas girls adapt quickly at this age. By 11 years old, many girls in traditional school systems are ahead of boys being more socially and intellectually attentive to the school environment. At adolescence however, some girls are vulnerable to losses in self-esteem, whereas boys may begin to find their footing physically, socially, and intellectually. Suddenly in early adolescence, girls must face sex role uncertainties just when the boys can begin to feel more capable in the school environment intellectually, socially, and physically. This can sometimes show up in slowing career aspirations for girls.[67]

Essentially, schools with "uniform" pedagogical strategies will affect girls and boys differentially during these periods of vulnerability. A wider variety of teaching methods and instructional settings could address and promote effective learning in each gender. This has potential to reduce behavioral conduct problems, alcohol and substance abuse, school violence, and early pregnancy. Currently, we lose children either through inattention during class, low attendance, drop out, or expulsion when school doesn't meet their individual learning needs.

In her invited guest article written for the January 29th, 2006 *Newsweek* issue entitled "Mommy I Know You," Psychologist and New York University Professor Carol Gilligan described an experience that her son had in his 2nd grade class during his vulnerable years. Apparently, the 2nd grade teacher had written, "Don't be afraid to ask," on the classroom blackboard. That same day, another young boy asked a question and was chastised by the teacher for asking a question. Apparently, Carol Gilligan's son called out, "Don't be afraid to ask!" perhaps attempting to restore justice in the classroom. The unexpected outcome for him was a sharp reprimand from the teacher. Carol Gilligan described what happened to her son as one example of how "[a] boy's intransigence, disruptiveness, indifference, or confrontation may instead be a refusal to engage in false relationship." Moreover, Gilligan explained, it is a characteristic of boys to "turn away from rather than seeking to repair or smooth over such ruptures as girls tend to do." Dr. Gilligan also said that, "this may explain why more boys disconnect from school. It also suggests, as my work with girls has shown, that an effective strategy for preventing boys' psychological difficulties and educational problems would involve recognizing their sensitivities, building honest relationships, and strengthening a healthy capacity for resistance."

In recent decades, there has been a debate[68] about separating boys and girls in different classrooms in public schools; the concept alone raises civil rights concerns about school segregation. The American Civil Liberties

Union[69] has actively opposed sex-segregated schools and questioned the relevance of neurological findings to school policy on sex segregation. Education research has not been able to settle the debate either, since aggregated results from studies on the success of gender segregated classrooms have produced mixed results.[70] In some situations, boys and girls can excel when taught differentially according to their gender needs,[71] sometimes not. Note that the outcome of any such study would depend on how success was actually measured, the complexity of learning obstacles within the school system and community (such as crime, discrimination, poverty), the classroom and school resources, teacher-student ratios, the dynamics of teacher-student-peer relationships, and more.[72]

Nonetheless advocates, such as Leonard Sax and Michael Gurian have influenced public school administrators with their publications and lectures.[73] In her article "Teaching Boys and Girls Separately" featured in the March 2nd 2008 *New York Times Magazine,* Elizabeth Weil noted that gender-segregated public schools had proliferated from two schools in 1995 to hundreds across the country in 2008. Despite the controversy, public schools around the country are making their choices.

Are there other ways to respect individual differences than classroom segregation by gender? Multiple intelligence theory[74] suggests that small changes in pedagogical approach can go a long way. Gregory and Chapman's 2002 book entitled, *Differentiated Instructional Strategies: One Size Doesn't Fit All,* suggested that variety in teaching methods as simple as having children work in pairs and in groups, can make a big difference in increasing opportunities for learning important concepts in multiple ways. Children have been found to be in clear agreement about this, preferring variety in instructional method, as noted in the Rosemarie Moore (author) and colleagues' report[75], *Dimensions of Learning for the Highly Gifted Student,* on an interview study conducted in the Palo Alto school district. Collaborative aspects of project work will support the development of emotional and social intelligence in both boys and girls. Teamwork in pairs and in groups, when led effectively by the teachers, also serves to reinforce the value of relational skills as a part of learning. Collaborative learning is just one example of alternative pedagogical approaches where children can learn about their individual strengths, while valuing the strengths of their partners in pairs or groups.

Whether classrooms are segregated by gender or not, a flexible school will support girls and boys in their special needs in the early years of school, engaging their efforts to achieve through teaching approaches suited to their needs and strengths. Similarly, a flexible school system can assist girls in their developmental needs and to understand themselves within a number of gender role definitions that include academic success, leadership qualities, and athletic ability in middle school years when they are vulnerable to declining belief in their potential. Varied instructional strategies can allow for differences in how boys and girls might respond to classroom methods and teacher and peer relationships.[76] Thereby, classroom arrangements and options can allow individuals in both genders a chance to thrive at their different stages of development.

One advantage of young inventors programs is that inventing itself is a complex endeavor. Invention engages children on different levels—physically, emotionally, and cognitively. Young inventor programs provide the opportunity for young children collaboratively to tinker with materials regularly, in an enjoyable and playful way, while practicing skills in inventive thinking, problem finding and solving.

Conclusion

Inventive, creative, and imaginative behavior begins early in a child's life in the home environment. In the home, warm mutual relationships between family members and communication with respect and encouragement for children can build skills and experiences for stable relationships in outside settings. Along with free time for imaginative play, clear and dependable home support can make a tremendous difference to a child's creative potential. The more children are actively and deeply engaged in school and home activities, the more likely they are to be reaping the optimal psychological, physical, and behavioral growth benefits to their overall development. The role of support and free play remains crucial to creativity into adulthood. Opportunities, such as young inventors programs, offer project learning that can be naturally paced to the individualized educational needs of the child, allowing them to thrive creatively at their full potential in at least one setting during the school week.

Further reading:

On the role of play in adult inventing:

Boyle, B. (2007, June 28). Ideas aren't cheap: Promoting the serious business of play: Better brainstorming is the key to innovation. *ABC News:* http://abcnews.go.com/Technology/Story?id=3323453&page=1

Brown, T. (2008, November). *Tim Brown: Tales of creativity and play*. Retrieved from: http://www.ted.com/talks/tim_brown_on_creativity_and_play.html

On creating environments that foster creativity and learning in children:

Alliance for childhood. (2006b). Fact Sheet: *Time for play, everyday*. Retrieved from: http://www.allianceforchildhood.org/publications

Ginsburg, K. R. (2007). The importance of play in promoting healthy child development and maintaining strong parent-child bonds. *Pediatrics, 119*(1), 182-191. Retrieved from: http://pediatrics.aappublications.org/content/119/1/182.full

Lundy, R. A., Carey, R. W., and Moore, R. K. (1977). *Dimensions of learning for the highly gifted student*. Palo Alto Unified School District.

Singer, D. G. and Singer, J. L. (2001). *Make-believe: Games and activities for imaginative play*. Washington DC: Magination Press.

Stipek, D. and Seal, K. (2001). *Motivated minds: Raising children to love learning: A practical guide to ensuring your child's success in school*. NY: Henry Holt & Co.

On children and media:

Singer, D. G. and Singer, J. L. (2005). *Imagination and play in the electronic age.* Cambridge, MA: Harvard University Press.

Singer, D. G. and Singer, J. L. (2007). *Handbook of children and the media.* Thousand Oaks, CA: Sage.

CHAPTER 4

What is the psychology behind invention?

Curiosity and learning in infancy

There is an unmistakable curiosity in children that parents observe as infants explore themselves, others, and nearly anything within reach.[77] Then as they 'hitch' and crawl, a new level of curious endeavor unfolds. This is matched by a new level of parent intention to manage these explorations with safety locks to cupboards and drawers.

What energizes such exploratory curiosity? Psychologists have developed various methods over the years to discover and study the abilities of very young children. The early observational studies by Jean Piaget in the 1920s showed that infants and young children actively learn through searching visually, listening, and exploring by touch. By mid-century, developmental research included study of perceptual integration, revealing how an infant's cognitive patterns involve all their senses (hearing, smell, taste, touch, sight) in their new learning. As the nature of a young child's developing mind became understood to include processing of information and actively organizing knowledge, the significance of social and material environments became significant for study.[78] From the 1950s forward, the role of the primary caregivers within the infant's learning and development became a hot field in psychology and in public interest.

Study of children's development today, especially with advances in neuroscience, gives a dynamic picture of attentive interest and exploration, relational needs, and rapid learning over time. During the first two years of infancy when the brain more than doubles in size, an infant's learning process is enhanced when the primary caregiver(s) and the extended family support system provide positive emotional responsiveness, challenge, and assistance with their developmental needs.[79] Allan Shore, a neuropsychology professor at the University of California Los Angeles' School of Medicine, has published and spoken widely on his perspectives from studying infant brain activity.[80] The bonding relationship between the primary caregiver(s) and the infant, Schore believed, has a profound effect on the infant's brain development. Those relational experiences build on each other at the neurocellular level as the brain grows and develops patterned neural concentrations.

As toddlers advance their exploratory endeavors in their environments, they use an increasing variety of cognitive strategies for understanding and integrating their past learning experiences.[81] Those who study the importance of the initial caregiver-infant bond suggest that those early warm, loving, and responsive relationships with primary caregivers and extended family support an infant and toddler's positive interests to interact with their environment and safely explore. This exploration in turn maximizes their cognitive learning opportunities through the early years when their physical brain is also growing rapidly.

What happens when toddlers start preschool?

Other psychologists, especially in the 1980s, evaluated the guiding role of family members, modeling influence of peers and siblings, and the role of teachers in supporting a child's learning. In particular, evidence mounted on the importance of having one primary teacher in each grade setting of the preschool through 2nd grade. Today, an optimal role of the primary teacher is one where he/she offers consistent interest, participation, and responsiveness to the child's learning and growing intellect. Another important dimension for early childhood school settings is to provide emotional comfort and encouragement during the daily learning process, and to support the child as an individual. In early grades, a primary teacher can also acknowledge the child's individual efforts in the learning process and celebrate his or her successes. With this primary influence in place, children are ready to adapt to other secondary teachers or instructional settings, such as art classes, physical education, parent helpers, and teaching assistants. The primary teacher has tremendous influence over how a child will embrace and express curiosity, creative development, and view their mistakes as important steps toward success.

What encourages a child's creative development?

In the 1980s, the role of *intrinsic* versus *extrinsic* motivation became understood as critical in fostering highly creative work. Extrinsic motivation is oriented toward receiving tangible material gain such as prizes, tokens, winning competitions, and money as compensation for doing the work, while intrinsic motivation involves emotionally based interest, enjoyment, satisfaction, and/or personal challenge in the work itself. The underlying notion in motivation theory[82] is that when offered extrinsic reward, one might be more likely to play it safe and make sure to do what is likely to meet the rewarded standards. If one engages in creative endeavor mainly for intrinsic reasons however, any creative leaps for the sake of originality, self-expression, and novelty in design could make the effort that much more rewarding. Have studies confirmed this theory?

Here is how Harvard Business School Professor Teresa Amabile discovered that a group of girls, aged 7-11, did respond differentially in their level of creative response when competing for (*extrinsic*) prizes versus (*intrinsic*) doing art for fun. The 1982 study[83] took place when Professor Amabile was at Brandeis University. She used an experimental design in an apartment complex where girls were invited to one of two art parties: one where girls were encouraged to make paper collages and told that three girls would be rewarded with prizes based on the quality of their art designs (*extrinsic*); in the other party (where the girls were encouraged to make paper collages), the girls were told that three among them would receive prizes raffled off according to the number on their name badge (i.e., independent of their collages—*intrinsic*).

Sure enough, the general raffle group produced significantly more creative collages than did the competition group. In terms of, "creativity," Ambile explained, "novel use of materials, variation in shapes, spontaneity, and complexity ... expert art raters were engaged to make the judgments on the quality of design. [The competition group] made collages that could be considered better-executed technically, in terms of organization, planning, and representationalism."[84] Dr Amabile's findings in this study suggested that material incentive, like competitive prizes, may motivate action but also may hinder creative risk-taking often vital to highly novel creativity.

What else influences creative achievement?

Similarly in the late 80s at the Stanford University School of Education, another psychology researcher Dr. Martin Ford[85] (now Senior Associate Dean at George Mason University) developed a model that explained motivation in a different way. In his 1992 book, *Motivating Humans: Goals, Emotions, and Personal Agency Beliefs*, Ford explained motivation to be influenced by:

- Beliefs about one's ability,
- Skill developed through practice, life experience, and educational knowledge,
- Emotional interest,
- Personal goals, and
- Environment (social, economic, and cultural), particularly in how the environment supports or hinders achievement.

This model can be illustrated through two hypothetical classroom scenarios. In the first scenario, imagine a 2nd grade classroom where the teacher is up at the chalkboard teaching spelling and asks the students if they know how to spell the word, *deciduous*. Manny shoots his hand up, thinking to himself: *Yes, I know the answer. I love spelling. I practice with my older sister every* day. Another student Samir hesitates, Hmmm. I'm not sure of the answer. I don't like spelling at all. My sister says I'm bad at spelling. No, I better not raise my hand. Manny and Samir have two different sets of thoughts, emotions, and behavior in reaction to the same stimuli.

In Manny's case, we know from his thoughts that he enjoys spelling (emotional interest), values learning (personal goal), has practiced spelling in a supportive relationship with her sister (developed skill in a supportive social environment), and most importantly, believes that he has the knowledge to answer the teacher's question (personal agency). The consequential behavior is that he throws up his hand enthusiastically (consequential behavior) to answer the question correctly (achievement).

In Samir's case, we can see from his thoughts that this child has not had the opportunity to practice spelling, has not experienced the satisfaction of spelling correctly, has been discouraged by her sister at home, and may not yet have experienced enough positive experiences to enjoy learning. The consequence is that Samir does not believe he has the knowledge to answer the teacher's question correctly, does not want to risk participation, and his hand stays down.

Martin Ford's motivation model is useful for narrowing down why a child might strive to achieve or not and affords us a trail map for investigating a situation holistically to find ways to restore that child's experience of learning, enjoyment of the endeavor, and belief in an ability to succeed. This may include working with the parent(s) to create a supportive environment to practice learning skills at home.

Below is hypothetical classroom scenario where a student Billy doesn't seem to be joining his peers in an art project and how Martin Ford's model could be useful in understanding some of what could be going on for the child.

Teacher: Billy, how about joining the other kids in creating animals with clay?

Billy: No, thank you. I'm tired.

Teacher (handing Billy some purple clay): Perhaps if you get started here with me, you might enjoy joining the other students in a few minutes.

Billy: I've never worked with clay before. I'm not good at art. My brother is really good. My mom says that he is the artist of the family.

Teacher: *OK, let's for now not worry about making animals. Let's just have fun. First let's you and me together smash our balls flat.*

[Billy follows the teacher, pounding his ball flat.]

Teacher: *Hmm, it looks like you have just accomplished making a pancake. Now, let's start at the side, and roll the pancake into a tube.*

Billy (showing a purple rolled tube): *OK, how's this?*

Teacher (holding her own yellow pancake tube): *Excellent, now let's do something daring. Let's roll the tube. How about if we start at one end of the tube, and roll, remembering to stop just before the end of the tube.*

Billy (rolling up the tube): *OK, like this?*

Teacher (leaning back to examine their products): *Yes, exactly like that. You know, Billy, I am spotting a snail here. How about you?*

Billy: *Oh, yeah.*

Teacher: *Now let's just add two little pieces at the tip of the roll. Snails need antennae to navigate where they are going.*

Billy: *Antennae? Oh yeah, I see.*

Teacher: *That's terrific, look at what we have accomplished, two snails. Let's go over and show the other students how to make snails.*

The story above is designed to show how Billy had developed the belief that he was not adept at art, certainly not as proficient as he had come to believe that his brother was. As his belief evolved, the thought of exposing this supposed lack of talent to his peer group became emotionally uncomfortable enough that Billy avoided art activities at school, thus forgoing the chance to practice and build skill in art. The astute teacher, wise to the influential nature of her role and to the fact that even one success experience can influence a child's belief system, encouraged Billy through a modeling process. The teacher's intuition was that Billy would learn quickly if she modeled for Billy an achievable way to practice making animals with clay and emotionally enjoy doing it. In the process of modeling, the teacher focused on tasks that Billy knew how to do, such as smashing clay flat and rolling tubes. By doing tasks that Billy knew how to do, she was able to help him create a snail, thereby giving Billy an enjoyable success experience while simultaneously learning the new skill of actually making a snail. Then capitalizing on the freshness of Billy's accomplishment, this astute teacher quickly facilitated Billy's re-entry with the other students. In this way, Billy could enjoy his sense of accomplishment in making snails, share his new treasure, and at the same time observe other students making clay animals and learn from their processes as well. This experience can then satisfy Billy's personal goal of acceptance, success, mastery, or enjoyment—whatever his unique personal goal may be.

How personal goals and emotions play into inventing?

When one observes a child highly engaged in a Lego project, what is going on for that child? Is it happiness in action? Intense thinking? What is really going on when a child, who normally can hardly sit still, becomes intensely involved in building a Lego's robot, drawing a picture, or searching for bugs? Furthermore, how is it that one child's enduring fascination with Spiderman is another child's passing fancy? Imagine how useful it would be if we could unlock these secrets. Think of it, difficult tasks could be transformed into interesting endeavor if we just knew how to frame the task to our young ones.

In his graduate years, Charles Nichols[86] (now a Clinical Psychologist in Georgia) joined Professor Martin Ford in the quest to explain in more detail the psychological concept of personal goals—a concept that refers to how and why people direct and organize their activity.[87] What is behind a person's choices in goal directed activity? Why does a person choose one activity over another? Perhaps more relevantly, why is one individual's delight another person's drudgery? After mastering the motivation literature and generating insights of their own, Ford and Nichols came up with a list of 24 goals (see Figure 10) that appear to direct and organize people's activity, which they called the *Taxonomy of Human Goals*.[88] Part of the usefulness of Ford and Nichols work on personal goals is that they are explained in terms of how they relate to a particular activity choice.

Figure 10: Taxonomy of Human Goals

For explanations for each of the 24 personal goals, see http://www.implicitself. com/index.php?cmd=apg.

For example, selecting two goals (stated as one) from Figure 10, *Resource Acquisition* and *Resource Provision* refer to activities such as, either *obtaining* or *providing* "support, assistance, advice, or validation from or to others". Imagine two young teenagers in the first week of training for a new crossing guard job: One individual has a personal goal of obtaining support, assistance, advice, or validation from others and therefore may enjoy being trained and coached on his new responsibilities for crossing guard. Another individual in this situation, who has the personal goal of providing support, assistance, advice, or validation to others, may feel impatient with the coaching and training process, looking forward when she can begin helping people cross the street safely. This example is intended to illustrate how, if we help young people understand their personal goals, we can help them anticipate what emotions they are likely to experience if we choose one activity over another.

The main thing to remember is that personal goals are quite different from task goals. So for example, a child may enjoy helping a parent bake a birthday cake for a neighbor. This activity may fit in with her personal goals of creativity and belonging, and involve many tasks goals, such as laying out the ingredients, mixing the batter, buttering the pan, preheating the oven. Personal goals, as conceived by Ford and Nichols, are not task goals but rather part of an internally generated motivation for persisting at an activity. So this individual's personal goals of creativity *and* belonging could both be satisfied by the one activity of making, decorating, and giving a gift of a cake to a neighborhood friend.

Both children and adults tend to pursue many activities, although individuals usually have a small set of important personal goals that they are seeking to satisfy, often unconsciously, in one form or another. An individual's personal goals tend to form early in childhood and stay more or less stable through life. So the more that teachers and parents can help young children understand themselves in terms of what activities they enjoy and why, the better children will be able to make satisfying choices in how they spend their time. Many types of activities can satisfy one particular personal goal.

How do we help young people discover their personal goals?

Both Martin Ford and Charles Nichols have come up with assessment tools to help teens and adults understand their goal structure. The Personal Goal Assessment[89] asks an individual about how how they would respond to a series of activities. These responses are then translated into the individual's likely personal goals. This latter assessment, right now free to the public, can be accessed at: http://www.implicitself.com/

What are the personal goals of inventors?

Studies on inventors, both early in the century and more recently (here in the U.S.[90] and in Europe[91]), asked inventors about why they did the inventing work that they did. The responses suggested a mix of intrinsic and extrinsic reasons, heavily weighted toward fulfillment of intrinsic personal goals first, such as challenge, mastery, enjoyment, and love for the inventing process. Many responses suggest that the inventing process was varied enough to satisfy different personal goals at any one time for different people. In Sheila Henderson's first study with inventors, a focus group conversation[92] went as follows:

> "It's all for the challenge," one inventor said, "to attempt to do something that people say can't be done." Another inventor looked over in complete disbelief, "Are you kidding? That's the worst part of the whole process. For me, it's the rush of solving the problem. Leaving a note on his [manager's] desk saying, 'It's solved!'" The third inventor said shaking is head, "I do this work because it saves lives. I love receiving the letters from people saying that a product that I make has saved their son or daughter's life!"

In Sheila Henderson's subsequent larger online survey of inventors,[93] the participants were also asked what motivated them to do inventing work. Ninety-nine percent of the inventor participants discussed *intrinsic* reasons, such as: "*I invent because it's fun.*" "*For the love of inventing.*" "*A way to improve the world.*"—similar to statements offered by inventors in Joseph Rossman's study in the early 1900s.

The role of emotion in creativity and invention

As we consider the role of emotion in creativity, think of a creative project in which you have recently engaged. When you began the activity, what part of the process did you look forward to the most? Did you enjoy thinking up and/or visualizing the idea? Or, were you most engaged by problem-solving on how to create the image that you had in your mind's eye? Or, did the moment of elation come for you when you actually figured it out? Did you enjoy more making the idea real? Were you a little disappointed after the endeavor was completed? For most people one stage of the process will appeal more than other stages; some stages will be excruciatingly difficult.

The nature of emotions and what generates emotions is a highly complex experience involving cognitive, neurological, physiological, endocrine, hormonal, and psychological processes. Perhaps because our emotions link so intensely with our physical body, negative emotions often get a particularly bad rap. Today's emphasis on being positive has devalued negative emotions for their usefulness to human life. Negative and positive emotions are generated in different parts of the brain, and both parts have important roles. Generally, the more parts of our brain that are engaged in an activity, the greater the benefits accrued for our brain development, learning, and for our creative and inventive success.

In Chapter 1, we discussed how annoyance can be a tremendous spark for creative action. There are two other ways that negative emotions can be useful during the inventing and designing process. First, negative emotion can be useful to us in affording us the opportunity to build important character strength for inventing. If one learns to work through concerns, fears and disappointments and still succeed, one can develop a certain mental tenacity and perseverance, which is a critical personality trait[94] for working on creative and inventive projects. In this way, negative emotion can be thought of as a frame to the joyful moments of success, much as a rainy day makes the next sunny day more delightful.

Second, negative emotions are critical signals in the inventive process. When one becomes frustrated that things are not moving forward, nothing seems to be making sense, everything is a blur, such frustration may be a signal for an important behavioral response—take a break. Sometimes by picking up an activity that is totally different, engaging a different part of the brain (such as taking a shower, getting some sleep, physical exercise, watching children play, reading a novel, drawing, cooking, etc.), an idea or a clarifying thought may seemingly come out of "nowhere."

Adults can help children develop openness to the array of human emotions and understanding for their usefulness. Children learn a lot by watching adults and their response to emotions. If adults are open to their range of emotions, the more likely children are to learn pro-social ways of expressing emotions to each other. The key to experiencing and expressing pro-socially a full range of emotional experience is to learn to regulate our behavioral response to our emotions, rather than block the emotions themselves. Adults can model this inclusive experience of emotions and also model pro-active regulation of their behavioral responses to them. Older family members can embrace feelings and each other in ways that build and maintain positive relationships. In turn the children are more likely to follow suit in recognizing and expressing the range of emotions and learning to regulate[95] their behavioral responses according to what they have observed.

Mihalyi Csikszentmihalyi, the author of the 1996 book, *Creativity: Flow and the Psychology of Discovery and Invention*, studied emotion during concentrated creative activity through a variety of experiments and personal interviews with highly creative people. What he described in his results was a state of emotional and cognitive flow[96] in the human experience. This flow state was later defined as the moments when the demands of a task exactly equal the highest level of one's skill and concentration. When an individual experiences this flow state, Csikszentmihalyi called this an *optimal experience*.

Some may relate to this experience of flow. Think back to one point when you might have been uniquely challenge by an activity, in such a way that you had the skills to accomplish the task but it required your complete focus. According to Csikszentmihalyi, if the activity is not challenging enough, one can get bored quickly; if the task demands surpass one's current level of skill, anxiety or frustration can result. The interesting thing is that many will talk about a sense of fulfillment that comes with simply being in this concentrated experience of flow. The fulfillment, however, comes after the event, not necessarily during the concentrated moments. *"Happiness,"* Csikszentmihalyi explained in speeches and in his 1990/2008 book *Flow,* "is derived from a series of flow moments over time."

The roller coaster of emotions in the invention process

Another psychologist and researcher Melvin P. Shaw was interested in the role of emotion *in engineering* and provided what may have been the first research evidence[97] that tolerating and enjoying the roller coaster of emotions was part of the inventing process. To do this research, Shaw interviewed a group of engineers about their process of technology development (otherwise termed in this book as *inventing*). What was novel was Melvin Shaw's inquiry of specifically how these engineers felt at different stages in the invention process. Through the information derived from these conversations, Shaw was able to map out emotions that were commonly felt at different stages of the creative process—a contribution to understanding the inner process of invention. IDEO, the design firm discussed in Chapter 1, uses a similar concept in what they call a *Mood Meter* designed to explain the potential for shifting emotions during the design process.

Consider the hypothetical scenario before where a teacher uses Sandra Russ' model to motivate a particularly bright young girl in her 4th grade class. In this case, the teacher looks over at Sarah who has finished her class work and is again napping with her head on the desk.

Teacher (tapping on her desk quietly, smiling): *Sarah, I have noticed that you are particularly fond of a good challenge.*

Sarah (looking up from her desk, yawning): *Uh, huh.*

Teacher: *I have been trying to think of a way to explain to our class, how a clock works? There is a website on how old wind up clocks work, but I think the class would enjoy seeing for themselves.*

Sarah: *Hmm.*

Teacher: *I wonder if you might be interested in helping with this project?*

Sarah: *Maybe…yes, I think so. Hmm, yes I would be.*

Teacher: *How about if you figure out how to take apart this old wind up clock and put it back together again? Meanwhile, I'll work on organizing a project for the class. If you are able to figure it out, I will see if I can find some more old wind up clocks so the other students can give it a try too.*

Sarah: *OK, I'll try.*

Teacher: *How about if you work on this over here at our inventors table. I wonder if you can do this without looking at the website?*

In this story, the teacher is accomplishing a number of things at once. First, the teacher has taken an interest in knowing Sarah and noticed that she seems particularly engaged (*emotion*) when she feels challenged (*personal goal*) by her schoolwork and appears rather bored (*emotion*) and sometimes disruptive (*behavior*) when she is not. Second, rather than commenting on Sarah's negative behavior, napping on her desk, the teacher helps Sarah to understand one of her personal goals (challenge) and reinforces this through positive acknowledgement. Third, the teacher expresses confidence in Sarah by offering her the special class task. By suggesting that they work in parallel rather than together, she offers Sarah both autonomy and support (additional potential *personal goals*). Fourth, by challenging Sarah to try disassembling and reassembling the clock on her own, the teacher will be able to learn more about Sarah's ability to persist through a challenge. Due to her knowledge about Csikszentmihalyi's optimal experience, she briefly mentions the website as a safety net, just in case she has overestimated Sarah's current level of problem solving skills.

Conclusion

In this chapter, we reviewed some of the psychology behind child development and inventive behavior. The topic of child development and human motivation is vast, so this chapter covers just a few useful theories in understanding children, and at the same time offers a few suggestions for ways to understand and prepare children optimally for inventing endeavor, both in their youth and as adults.

Further reading

On child development:

Gopnik, A., Meltzolff, A. N., Kuhl, P. K. (2001). *The scientist in the crib: What early learning tells us about the mind*. NY: Harper Perennial.

Waters, R. (2004, November 14). The Baby Brain Connection: Armed with new research on developing brain structure, social workers can help fix troubled baby/parent relationships. *The San Francisco Chronicle*. Sunday paper. Retrieved at: http://www.sfgate.com/health/article/The-Baby-Brain-Connection-Armed-with-new-2672397.php

On assessments of motivation:

Henderson, S. J. (2009). Assessment of personal goals: An online tool for personal counseling, coaching, and business consulting. *Measurement and Evaluation in Counseling and Development, 41*, 244-249.

As mentioned above, the *Personal Goal Assessment* is free to the public available through: http://www.implicitself.com/

On flow, creativity, and optimal experience:

Csikszentmihalyi, M. (1990, 2008). *Flow: The psychology of optimal experience*. NY: Harper Perennial.

Csikszentmihalyi, M. (1996). *Creativity: Flow and the psychology of discovery and invention*. NY: Harper Perrenial.

Conclusion

In April 2004, there was a gathering in Washington D.C., a two-day conference reporting on a year-long task force review of American invention. The mission of the gathering was to inspire researchers, writers, educators, and politicians toward a vision for invention in the 21st century. "We live in a historical moment concerning the development of invention and its impact on quality of life,"[98] wrote Merton C. Flemings, Professor Emeritus at Massachusetts Institute of Technology. "…Creativity is a central source of the meaning of human life." Professor Flemings explained,[99] "Most things that are interesting, important, and human are the results of creativity." While the urge to explore may be innate, inventiveness is a result of learning. Research in psychology and engineering suggest strongly that early experiences with inquiry, discovery, problem-solving, creativity, ingenuity, and inventing are the fundamental building blocks for highly creative accomplishments in adulthood. Why inventing per se? "Technical invention contrasts with scientific inquiry in its focus on developing things that fulfill practical functions," Flemings said.[100] People who invent have two qualities that stand out among their array of knowledge and abilities: First, they have an uncanny ability to discern the core problems of our culture. Second, they apply their hard earned talents and knowledge to deliver solutions that work. Their solutions work by allowing us to adapt positively to change.

One question is: Are we fostering the kind of inventive minds in our children and young adults that we will need to meet the challenges ahead? Early and secondary education in the United States has inherent problems that go far beyond lack of funding. The disconcerting levels of boredom, disengagement, and drop out pervading our schools are symptoms of larger systemic problems. Primary and secondary education needs novel opportunities for young school children that will foster inventive and creative behavior at home and at school.

The central question in our book was: *How can we as parents, educators, and administrators collaborate together to foster and channel the inventive spirit in young children towards a lifetime of positive, responsible, and productive achievement?* We addressed this question by showcasing stories about individuals who have invented early in their lives, sharing what adult inventors have discussed about their childhood experiences with invention, and explained psychological theory behind invention, creativity, and play. Then in a sequel to this book, *Invention Friday Curriculum*, we offer a step-by-step les-son plan series with evaluation tools to monitor children according to their learning progress along the multiple intelligence categories.

The goal of this book is to make it a little easier for a parent or volun-teer to bring an "Invention Friday" program to a school in the classroom or after school, and/or taught by parents at home. The "Invention Friday" lesson series is one way that parents and families can increase opportuni-ties for children to discover their inventive talent within the existing sys-tem of education. Teachers, parents, administrators, along with community and business leaders can initiate programs within the existing structure for profound impact on how children view their role in this next century. The "Invention Friday" series of learning activities is a program that parents can help teachers implement fairly easily.

The spirit of inventiveness has been universally alive for centuries. Anesthesia, antibiotics, democracy, the Bill of Rights, bicycles, electric cars, neurosurgery, the United Nations, Apollo 13, sliced bread, silly putty, Montessori schools, solar heating, and microwave technologies are all exam-ples of human inventiveness. Along with adults, children have been inventing for at least one century, probably longer. There is little available data on how many children have devised clever inventions and been awarded US patents, but many fascinating anecdotes abound about kid inventors.

Our goal for this book has been to provide an impetus for parents and teachers to provide opportunities for children to invent in school, in clubs, and at home. Upon turning the last page of this book, we hope that our readers will have come to value the "spirit of inventiveness." Mihalyi Csikszentmihalyi in his 1990 book *Flow: The psychology of optimal experience*, said that, "We create ourselves by how we invest our energy." We argue that all of us create our future by how we invest in our children's life ex-periences. Invention is crucial to support the fundamental human need for stability, consistency, and predictability. Our book seeks to address this wis-dom directly by offering ways for interested adults to guide the creative energies of children into productive inventive adults clearly needed to carry us through the 21st century.

Endnotes

⚡ Authors' note

[1] For more information see: *Meant to Invent! Teacher Guide. "Why invent?"* American Academy of Sciences. Young Inventors Program. Retrieved from http://www.aas-world.org/ (Note: AAS had a previous publication entitled, *Why Invent?*).

[2] For more information see http://www.sciencefriday.com/

⚡ Chapter 1: What does it mean to be an inventor?

[3] See in bibliography, Flatow, 1993; Giblin, 1987; Weber, 1992.

[4] See Frederick McKinley Jones (1893-1961). (1996-2008). *Black History Pages.* 5x5 Media and African Images. Retrieved from: http://www.blackhistorypages.net/pages/fjones.php

[5] See in bibliography, Kemper, 2003.

[6] For a description of the Ultimate Utility Bike designed by IDEO for Oregon Manifest, see http://www.ideo.com/work/faraday-bike/

[7] For The Foundry incubator, see: http://www.thefoundry.com/

[8] Edward Zigler, a Sterling Professor Emeritus of Psychology at Yale University, was one of the original planners and founders of Project Head Start for which he received the Heinz Award in Public Policy and the Award for Outstanding Lifetime Contribution to Psychology. See http://www.heinzawards.net/recipients/edward-zigler

[9] See publications authored by Tim Brown at IDEO at http://www.ideo.com/people/tim-brown

[10] This definition of invention is derived from prior definitions of both creativity and invention in psychology and product design literature. In bibliography, see: Amabile, 1983; Becker, 1994; Faste, 1972; MacKinnon, 1962; Rossman, 1964; Weber, 1992.

[11] See in bibliography: Brown, 2008.

[12] This chapter can be found in Shaw & Runco, 1994, in bibliography.

[13] For more on this see Chapter 3: Innovation begins with an eye in Brown with Littman, 2001, in bibliography.

[14] For more on qualities and characteristics of creative and inventive people, see in bibliography: Brown, 2008; Russ, 1993/1999.

[15] Problem-finding is a concept widely discussed in "best practices" on inventing and long used in the training of engineers in Stanford University's Product Design program and the Stanford University Hasso Plattner Institute of Design (D-School). In bibliography, see Faste, 1972.

[16] In bibliography, see Getzels and *Csikszentmihalyi*, 1976.

[17] For good happenstance stories in invention, see in bibliography: Jones, 1994/1998: Roberts, 1989; Royston & Roberts, 1994.

[18] In bibliography, see Henderson, 2000.

[19] For more on "bug" lists, see in bibliography: Brown with Littman, 2001, p. 28.

[20] See "A child's eye" on p. 33 of Brown with Littman, 2001, in bibliography. Also see, *Understand mixtape: Discovering insights via human engagement*, offered by the Stanford Design School, retrieved at: http://dschool.stanford.edu/dgift/#gear-up

[21] See Chapter 6, p. 101 of Brown with Littman, 2001, in bibliography. Also see, *Experiment mixtape: Advancing your solution via prototyping*, offered by the Stanford Design School, retrieved at: http://dschool.stanford.edu/dgift/#gear-up

[22] In bibliography, see Tucker, 1995.

[23] There is a National Stuttering Association that has established local support groups for people who stutter to get peer support that can be vital to their self-esteem and self-empowerment process.

[24] See "A child's eye" on p. 33 of Brown with Littman, 2001, in bibliography. Also see, *Understand mixtape: Discovering insights via human engagement*, offered by the Stanford Design School, retrieved at: http://dschool.stanford.edu/dgift/#gear-up

[25] For more on Dr. Charles Drew, see: http://www.web.mit.edu/invent/iow/cdrew.html

[26] For more on the author's inventor research, see: Henderson, 2002/2004a/2004b.

[27] See in bibliography, Guiri et al., 2007.

[28] See in bibliography, Amesse, Desranleau, Etemad, Fortier, & Seguin-Dulude, 1991; Beauchamp & McDaniel, 1990;

[29] See in bibliography, MacDonald, 1986.

[30] See in bibliography, Guiri et al., 2007.

[31] For more on Mary Anderson, see in bibliography, Thimmesh, 2000.

[32] For more on astronaut Ellen Ochoa, see: http://www.invention.smithsonian.org/centerpieces/ilives/lecture07.html

[33] For more on Judy W. Reed, see: US Patent and Trademark Office (2002, February 16th). Press Release: USPTO recognizes inventive women during Women's History Month. Retrieved from: http://www.uspto.gov/news/pr/2002/02-16.jsp

[34] For more on Sarah Goode, see: http://www.blackpast.org/?q=aah/goode-sarah-e-c-1855-1905

[35] See in bibliography, Flatow, 1993.

[36] For more on Thomas Edison, see in bibliography: Conot, 1986.

[37] See in bibliography Hirsch, Kett, & Trefil, 2002.

⸘ Chapter 2: Who says children are too young to invent?

[38] See in bibliography, Schlesinger, 1987a/1987b/1982.

[39] Phone conversation on July 16, 2003 with Ruth Nybold at the United States Patent and Trademark Office.

[40] As mentioned in Chapter 1, Joseph Rossman's study of inventors in the early 1900's, 20 inventor respondents indicated that they had made their first invention between five to nine years old. Four participants indicated that they had made their most important invention at ages 15-19. See in bibliography, Rossman, 1964.

[41] Phone conversation and an email dated 7/25/03 with Ruth Nyblod from the US Patent and Trademark Office.

[42] The story about Jacob Dunnack and his invention, featured by The Great Idea Finder website, was last retrieved on November 26, 2008: http://www.ideafinder.com/history/inventions/jdbatball.htm

[43] For the story of Wang Yani and her art, see in bibliography Zhensun, & Low, 1991.

[44] See in bibliography, Kindler, 1997.

[45] P. 48 in Davis, J. (1997). The "U" and the wheel of "C." In Kindler, A.M. (Ed). *Child development in art.* Reston, VA: National Art Education Association. Also see in bibliography, Davis, 1997b.

[46] For more information on John Ruggieri work, see website retrieved on November 26, 2008: http://johnruggieri.com/artpublic.htm See http://johnruggieri.com/ In bibliography, see Springen, 2000.

4   7

Springen, K. (2000). "Get Your Fingers into Art," Newsweek/SCORE.

[48] Silander, L. (1999). "Refrigerator art revisited," Rhode Island School of Design Views, Summer.

[49] See in bibliography, Henderson, 2002/2004a/2004b.

[50] See in bibliography, Singer, 1998a/1998b.

51 See in bibliography, Henderson, 2002/2004a/2004b. In particular, for a discussion of the role of fantasy in inventing, see Henderson, 2004a, p. 303.

52 See the InnovEd young inventor program in Mauritius at: http://www.gov.mu/portal/sites/nsp/popular/gscience.htm

Chapter 3: Support, play, and respect for individual differences

53 In bibliography, see Russ, 2003, p. 98.

54 In bibliography, see Harrington, Block, & Block, 1987.

55 In bibliography, see Ambile, 1989; Finnerty, 2005; Ginsburg, 2007; Singer, 1989a/1989b; Singer & Singer, 1990/2001/2005/2007/2009.

56 In bibliography, see Singer, 1989a/1989b; Singer & Singer, 1990/2001/2005/2007/2009.

57 In bibliography, see Stipek & Seal, 2001.

58 In bibliography, see Alliance for Childhood, 2006a.

59 In bibliography, see Alliance for Childhood, 2006b.

60 In bibliography, see Hart, 2002.

61 In bibliography, see Singer & Singer, 2005/2007.

62 See Article 31 in Office of the United Nations High Commissioner for Human Rights. Convention on the Rights of the Child. General Assembly Resolution 44/25 of 20 November 1989. Retrieved from: http://www2.ohchr.org/english/law/crc.htm

63 In bibliography, see Ginsburg, 2007.

64 In bibliography, see Stanberry, 2008a.

65 In bibliography, see Weil, 2008.

66 In bibliography, see Gilligan, 2006; Stanberry, 2008a; Weil, 2008.

67 In bibliography, see Watson, Quatman, & Elder, 2002.

[68] For information on the sex-segregated schools debate, see in bibliography: Balkin, 2002; Stanberry, 2008b.

[69] In bibliography, see ACLU, 2008.

[70] In bibliography, see Mael, Alonso, Gibson, Rogers, & Smith, 2005; Weil, 2008.

[71] In bibliography, see Tyre, 2006.

[72] For more on the possible effects of the school system on study results, see in bibliography: Watson, Quatman, & Elder, 2002.

[73] In bibliography, see Gurian, 2002; Sax, 2006.

[74] For more on multiple intelligences, see in bibliography: Bellanca, Chapman, & Swartz, 1997; Campbell, Campbell, & Dickinson, 2004; Teacher Created Resources Staff, 1999.

[75] In bibliography, see Lundy, Carey, & Moore, 1977.

[76] In bibliography, see: Lundy, Carey, & Moore, 1977.

Chapter 4: What is the psychology behind invention?

[77] In bibliography, see Stipek & Seal, 2001.

[78] In bibliography, see Gibson, 1969.

[79] In bibliography, see Gibson, 1969; Waters, 2004.

[80] In bibliography, see Shore, 1999. For more on Allan Schore's publications, see: http://www.allanschore.com/

[81] In bibliography, see Gopnik, Meltzolff, & Kuhl, 2001.

[82] In bibliography, see Amabile, 1982/1983/1989; Koestner, & Ryan, 2001; Ryan & Deci, 2000.

[83] In bibliography, see Amabile, 1982.

[84] In bibliography, see Amabile, 1982, p. 576.

[85] For more on Martin E. Ford, PhD, see: http://www.implicitself.com/index.php?cmd=authors

86 For more on Charles W. Nichols, PhD, see: http://www.implicitself.com/index.php?cmd=authors

87 In bibliography, see Ford & Nichols (1987).

88 For more information on the Taxonomy of Personal Goals, see: http://www.implicitself.com/index.php?cmd=takeAPG

89 For more information of the online Personal Goal Assessment, see: http://www.implicitself.com/index.php?cmd=takeAPG

90 See in bibliography, Henderson, 2002/2004a/2004b.

91 See in bibliography, Guiri et al., 2007.

92 For more on this study, see: Henderson, 2004a/2004b.

93 In bibliography, see Henderson 2004b/2002.

94 In bibliography, see Russ, 1993.

95 See Professor James Gross at Stanford University discuss emotion regulation at: http://vimeo.com/43421746 and also see in bibliography, Gross, 2007.

96 For more on flow, see in bibliography, Csikszentmihalyi, 1990/2008.

97 In bibliography, see Shaw, 1989.

Conclusion

98 See in bibliography, *Invention: Enhancing inventiveness for quality of life, competitiveness, and sustainability,* 2004, p. 11.

99 See in bibliography, *Invention: Enhancing inventiveness for quality of life, competitiveness, and sustainability,* 2004, p. 8.

100 See in bibliography, *Invention: Enhancing inventiveness for quality of life, competitiveness, and sustainability,* 2004, p. 14.

Bibliography

Adams, J. L. (1972). Individual and small group creativity. *Engineering Education, 63*(2), 100-105, 131.

Alliance for Childhood (2006a). *The importance of play: children from birth to five.* A statement of first principles on early education for educators and policymakers. Available upon request from: http://www.allianceforchildhood.org

Alliance for childhood. (2006b). Fact sheet: *Time for play, everyday.* Retrieved from: http://www.allianceforchildhood.org/publications

Amabile, T. M. (1989). *Growing up creative: Nurturing a lifetime of creativity.* Buffalo, NY: Creative Education Foundation Press.

Amabile, T. M. (1983). *The social psychology of creativity.* NY: Springer-Verlag.

Amabile, T. M. (1982). Children's artistic creativity: Detrimental effects of competition in a field setting. *Personality and Social Psychology Bulletin, 8*(3), 573-578.

American Civil Liberties Union (2008). *Sex segregated schools: separate and unequal.* Retrieved from: http://www.aclu.org/womensrights/edu/30129res20070614.html

Amesse, F., Desranleau, C., Etemad, H., Fortier, Y., & Seguin-Dulude, L. (1991). The individual inventor and the role of entrepreneurship: A survey of the Canadian evidence. *Research Policy, 20*(1), 13-27.

Balkin, Jack M. (2002). Is there a slippery slope from single-sex education to single-race education? *The Journal of Blacks in Higher Education, 37,* 126.

Beauchamp, R. S., & McDaniel, S. A. (1990). Women inventors in Canada: Research and intervention. In Marianne G. Ainley (Ed.), *Despite the odds: Essays on Canadian women and science* (pp. 304-315). Montreal, Quebec: Véhicule

Press. Retrieved from: http://content.lib.utah.edu/cdm/ref/collection/uspace/id/4561

Becker, G.M. (1994). Making it or finding it. In M. P. Shaw and M.A. Runco (Eds.) (1994). *Creativity and affect* (pp. 168-180). Norwood, NJ: Ablex Publishing.

Bellanca, J., Chapman, C., and Swartz, E. (1997). *Multiple assessments for multiple intelligences,* 3rd Ed. Thousand Oaks, CA: Corwin Press.

Boyle, B. (2007, June 28th). Ideas aren't cheap: Promoting the serious business of play: Better brainstorming is the key to innovation. *ABC News.* Retrieved from: http://abcnews.go.com/Technology/Story?id=3323453&page=1

Borges, P. (2007). *Women empowered.* NY: Rizzoli.

Brown, T. (2008, June). Design thinking. *Harvard Business Review.* For more publications by Tim Brown, see: Tim Brown at IDEO at http://www.ideo.com/people/tim-brown

Brown, T. with Littman, J. (2001). *The art of innovation: Lessons in creativity from IDEO.* NY: Doubleday.

Camhi, L. (2006, June 18th). If a little genius lives in the house, what's on the fridge? *The New York Times,* Art Section, p. 34.

Campbell, L., Campbell, B., & Dickinson, D. (2004). *Teaching and learning through multiple intelligences,* 3rd Ed. Boston: Pearson Education.

Caney, S. (1991). *The invention book.* NY: Workman Publishing.

Cassidy, J. (1999). The nature of a child's ties. In J. Cassidy & P. R. Shaver (Eds.), *Handbook of attachment theory, research, and clinical applications* (pp.3-20). NY: Guilford Press.

Cassidy, J. & Shaver, P. R. (Eds.) (1999). *Handbook of attachment theory, research, and clinical applications.* NY: Guilford Press.

Chapman, C. & King, R. (2007). *Differentiated instructional strategies for reading in the content areas,* 2nd Ed. Thousand Oaks, CA: Corwin Press.

Conot, R. (1986). *Thomas A. Edison: A streak of luck.* Cambridge, MA: Da Capo Press.

Csikszentmihalyi, M. (1990, 2008). *Flow: The psychology of optimal experience.* NY: Harper Perennial.

Csikszentmihalyi, M. (1996). *Creativity: Flow and the psychology of discovery and invention.* NY: Harper Perrenial.

Davis, J. (2008). *Why our schools need the arts.* NY: Teachers College Press.

Davis, J. (1997a). The "U" and the wheel of "C." In Kindler, A. M. (Ed). *Child development in art.* Reston, VA: National Art Education Association.

Davis, J. H. (1997b). The what and the whether of the U: Cultural implications of understanding development in graphic symbolization. *Human Development, 40*(3), 145-154.

Davis, J. H. (2008). *Why our schools need the arts.* NY: Teachers College Press.

Deci, E. L., Koestner, R., & Ryan, R. M. (2001). Extrinsic rewards and intrinsic motivation in education: Reconsidered once again. *Review of Educational Research, 71,* 1-27.

Dunn, J. (1994). *Tricks of the trade for kids.* Boston: Houghton Mifflin.

Egan, L. H. (1997). *Inventors and inventions.* NY: Scholastic Professional Books.

Eisner, E. (1998). *The kind of schools we need.* Westport, CT: Greenwood Press.

Ericsson, K. A., Charness, N., Feltovich, P. J., & Hoffman, R. R. (Eds.) (2006). *The Cambridge Handbook of Expertise and Expert Performance.* NY: Cambridge University Press.

Erlbach, A. (1997). *The Kids' Invention Book.* Minneapolis, MN: Lerner Publishing Group.

Faste, R. (1972). The role of visualization in creative behavior. *Engineering Education, 63*(2), 124-127.

Fineberg, J. (1997). *The innocent eye: Children's art and the modern artist.* Princeton, NJ: Princeton University Press.

Finnerty, K. O. (2005). Celebrating the creativity of the young child. *Journal of Museum Education. 30*(4), 9-13.

Flatow, I. (1993). *They all laughed . . . from light bulbs to lasers: The fascinating stories behind the great inventions that have changed our lives.* NY: Harper Collins.

Ford, M. E. (1992). *Motivating humans: goals, emotions, and personal agency beliefs.* Thousand Oaks, CA: Sage.

Ford, M. E., & Nichols, C. W. (1987). A taxonomy of human goals and some possible applications. In M. E. Ford & D. H. Ford (Eds.), *Humans as self-constructing living systems: Putting the framework to work* (pp. 289-311). Hillsdale, NJ: Lawrence Erlbaum.

Frederick McKinley Jones (1893-1961). (1996-2008). *Black history pages.* Retrieved from: http://www.blackhistorypages.net/pages/fjones.php

Getzels, J. W. & Csikszentmihalyi, M. (1976). *The creative vision: A longitudinal study of problem finding in art.* NY: Wiley.

Giblin, J. C. (1987). *From hand to mouth, Or, how we invented knives, forks, spoons, and chopsticks, & the table manners to go with them.* NY: Harper Collins.

Gibson, E. J. (1969). *Principles of perceptual learning and development.* Englewood Cliffs, NJ: Prentice Hall.

Gilligan, C. (2006, January 29th). Mommy, I know you. *Newsweek.* Retrieved from: http://www.newsweek.com/id/47523

Ginsburg, K. R. (2007). The importance of play in promoting healthy child development and maintaining strong parent-child bonds. *Pediatrics, 119*(1), 182-191. Retrieved from: http://pediatrics.aappublications.org/content/119/1/182.full

Giuri, P., Mariani, M., Brusoni, S. Crespi, G., Francoz, D., Gambardella, A., Garcia-Fontes, W., Geuna, A., Gonzalez, R., Harhoff, D., Hoisl, K., Le Bas, C., Luzzi, A., Magazzini, L., Nesta, L., Nomaler, O., Palomeras, N., Patel, P., Romanelli, M., & Verspagen, B. (2007). Inventors and invention processes in Europe: Results from the PatVal-EU survey. *Research Policy 36,* 1107–1127.

Gopnik, A. (2002, September 20th). Bumping into Mr. Ravioli. *The New Yorker.*

Gopnik, A., Meltzolff, A. N., & Kuhl, P. K. (2001). *The Scientist in the crib: What early learning tells us about the mind.* NY: Harper Perennial.

Gregory, G. H., & Chapman, C. M. (2002). *Differentiated instructional strategies: One size doesn't fit all.* Thousand Oaks, CA: Sage.

Gross, J. J. (Ed.) (2007). *Handbook of emotion regulation.* NY: Guilford Press.

Guinness World Records. (1999). *Guinness book of the 20th century: Millennium edition,* North Salem, NY: Mint Publishers.

Gurian, M. (2002). *Boys and girls learn differently! A guide for teachers and parents.* NY: Jossey-Bass.

Harper, C. M. (2001). *Imaginative inventions.* London: Little, Brown, & Co.

Harrington, D. M., Block, J. H., & Block, J. (1987). Testing aspects of Carl Rogers' theory of creative environments: Child-rearing antecedents of creative potential in young adolescents. *Journal of Personality and Social Psychology, 52,* 851-856.

Hart, T. (2002, December-February). Break out of the Box: Television and medias effect on our kids. *Byron Child: A Magazine for Progressive Adults,* 4.

Henderson, S. J. (2009). Assessment of Personal Goals: An online tool for personal counseling, coaching, and business consulting. *Measurement and Evaluation in Counseling and Development, 41,* 244-249. Available at: Available at: http://www.researchgate.net/profile/Sheila_Henderson/publications/

Henderson, S. J. (2004a). Product inventors and creativity: The finer dimensions of enjoyment. *Creativity Research Journal.* 16(2 & 3), 103-126. Available at: http://www.researchgate.net/profile/Sheila_Henderson/publications/

Henderson, S. J. (2004b). Inventors: The ordinary genius next door. In R. J. Sternberg, E. L. Grigorenko, & J.L. Singer (Eds.), *Creativity: from potential to realization* (pp. 293-312). Washington DC: American Psychological Assoc. Available at: http://www.researchgate.net/profile/Sheila_Henderson/publications/

Henderson, S. J. (2002). *Correlates of inventor motivation, creativity, and achievement.* Doctoral dissertation, Stanford University. Dissertation

Abstracts International. Available at: http://www.researchgate.net/profile/ Sheila_Henderson/publications/

Henderson, S. J. (2000). Creative innovation courses: Forums for personal growth and career exploration. Unpublished manuscript.

Hérbert, T. P., Karnes, F. A., & Stephens, K. R. (2005). *Inventions and inventing for gifted students.* Austin, TX: Prufrock Press.

Hirsch, Jr., E. D., Kett, J. F., & Trefil, J. (Eds.) (2002). *The new dictionary of cultural literacy*, 3rd Ed. Boston: Houghton Mifflin.

Invention: Enhancing inventiveness for quality of life, competitiveness, and sustainability. (2004). Report of the committee for study of invention. Retrieved from: http://web.mit.edu/invent/report.html

Jones, C. F. (1998). Accidents *may happen: Fifty inventions discovered by mistake.* NY: Delacorte Press.

Jones, C. F. (1994). *Mistakes that worked: 40 familiar inventions and how they came to be.* NY: Delacorte Press.

Kemper, S. (2003). *Code name ginger: The story behind Segway and Dean Kamen's quest to invent a new world.* Cambridge, MA: Harvard Business School Press.

Kepler, L. (1997, March). Tired of the age old science fair? Put on a science celebration. *Instructor-Intermediate, 106*(6), 59.

Kindler, A. M. (1997). *Child development in art.* Reston, VA: National Art Education Association.

Lautz, S. (2001). *What are the steps in setting up a successful science fair?* On the Website entitled, A science fair handbook for teachers, parents, and students. Retrieved from: http://mset.rst2.edu/portfolios/l/lautz_s/ Science%20Fair%20Handbook/Settingupfair.html

Love, S. (1977). *One blood: The death and resurrection of Charles R. Drew.* Chapel Hill, NC: University of North Carolina Press.

Lundy, R. A., Carey, R. W., & Moore, R. K. (1977). *Dimensions of learning for the highly gifted student.* Palo Alto, CA: Palo Alto Unified School District.

Mael, F., Alonso, A., Gibson, D., Rogers, K., & Smith, M. (2005). *Single-sex versus coeducational schooling: A systematic review.* Report prepared for the Department of Education. Washington DC: American Institute of Research. Retrieved from: http://www.ed.gov/rschstat/eval/other/single-sex/index.html

MacDonald, S. (1986). The distinctive research of the individual inventor. *Research Policy, 15*(4), 199-210.

McCormack, A. J. (1984, March-April). Teaching inventiveness. *Childhood Education,* 249-255.

McCormack, A. J. (1981). *Inventors workshop.* Belmont, CA: Pitman Learning.

MacFarquhar, L. (1999, December 6th). Looking for trouble: How an inventor gets his best ideas. *The New Yorker,* 78-93.

Ott, M. V. and Swanson, G. M. (1994). *I've got an idea!: The story of Frederick McKinley Jones.* Minneapolis, MN: Runestone Press.

Roberts, R. M. (1989). *Serendipity: Accidental discoveries in science.* NY: John Wiley & Sons.

Rossman, J. (1935). A study of childhood, education and age of 710 inventors. *Journal of the Patent Office Society, XVII*(5), 411-.

Rossman, J. (1964). *Industrial creativity: The psychology of the inventor.* New Hyde Park, NY: University Books.

Royston, M. & Roberts, J. (1994). *Lucky science: Accidental discoveries from gravity to velcro, with experiments.* NY: John Wiley & Sons.

Runco, M.A. (1994). Creativity and its discontents. In M. P. Shaw & M.A. Runco (Eds.) *Creativity and affect* (pp. 102-123). Norwood, NJ: Ablex Publishing Corp.

Runco, M. A. (1999). Tension, adaptability, and creativity. In S. W. Russ (Ed.), *Affect, creative experience, and psychological adjustment* (pp. 165-194). Philadelphia, PA: Brunner/Mazel.

Russ, S.W. (Ed.) (1999). *Affect, creative experience, and psychological adjustment.* Philadelphia, PA: Brunner/Mazel.

Russ, S.W. (1993). *Affect and creativity:The role of affect and play in the creative process*. Hillsdale, NJ: Lawrence Erlbaum.

Ryan, R. M., & Deci, E. L. (2000). Intrinsic and extrinsic motivations: Classic definitions and new directions. *Contemporary Educational Psychology, 25*, 54-67.

Sapolsky, R. M. (2004). *Why Zebras Don't Get Ulcers*. NY: Owl Books.

Sax, L. (2006). *Why gender matters:What parents and teachers need to know about the emerging science of sex differences*. NY: Broadway Books.

Shaw, M. P. & Runco, M. A. (Eds.) (1994). *Creativity and affect*. Norwood, NJ: Ablex Publishing.

Shaw, M. P. (1989).The Eureka process:A structure for the creative experience in science and engineering. *Creativity Research Journal, 2,* 286-298.

Shlesinger, Jr., B. E. (1987a). *How to invent:A text for teachers and students*. NY: Plenum Books.

Schlesinger, Jr., B. E. (1987b). Teaching problem-solving through invention. *Vocational Education Journal, 62*(5), 36-37.

Schlesinger, Jr., E.B. (1982). An untapped resource of inventors: Gifted and talented children. *The Elementary School Journal, 82*(3), 215-220.

Shore, A. (1999). *Affect regulation and the origin of the self*. Hillsdale, NJ: Lawrence Erlbaum.

Silander, L. (1999, Summer). Refrigerator art revisited. *Rhode Island School of Design Views*.

Simonton, D. (1999). *Origins of genius:Darwinian perspectives on creativity*. NY: Oxford University Press.

Singer, J. L. (1998a). Imaginative play in early childhood: A foundation for adaptive emotional and cognitive development. *International Medical Journal, 5*(2), 93-100.

Singer, J. L. (1998b). Daydreams, the stream of consciousness, and self-representations. In R. Bornstein & J. Masling (Eds.), *Empirical perspectives on the psychoanalytic unconsciousness* (pp. 141-186).Washington DC:APA Books.

Singer, D. G. & Singer, J. L. (2009). Children's pastimes and play in sixteen nations: Is free play declining? *American Journal of Play, 1*(4).

Singer, D. G. & Singer, J. L. (2007). *Handbook of children and the media.* Thousand Oaks, CA: Sage.

Singer, D. G. & Singer, J. L. (2005). *Imagination and play in the electronic age.* Cambridge, MA: Harvard University Press.

Singer, D. G. & Singer, J. L. (2001). *Make-believe: Games and activities for imaginative play.* Washington DC: Magination Press.

Singer, D. G. & Singer, J. L. (1990). *The house of make-believe: Children's play and the developing imagination.* Cambridge, MA: Harvard University Press.

Springen, K. (2000). *Get your fingers into art.* Newsweek/SCORE.

Stanberry, K. (2008a). *Girls' and boys' brains: How different are they?* Retrieved from: http://www.greatschools.net/cgi-bin/showarticle/3613?cpn=popArticl esAD_boysandgirlslearn

Stanberry, K. (2008b). *Single-sex education: The pros and cons.* Retrieved from: http://www.greatschools.net/cgi-bin/showarticle/3649

Sternberg, R. J. (Ed.). (1999). *Handbook of creativity.* NY: Cambridge University Press.

Sternberg, R. J., Grigorenko, E. L., & Singer, J. L. (Eds.) (2004). *Creativity: from potential to realization.* Washington DC: American Psychological Association.

Stipek, D. & Seal, K. (2001). *Motivated Minds: Raising children to love learning: A practical guide to ensuring your child's success in school.* NY: Henry Holt.

Taylor, M. (2001). *Imaginary companions and the children who create them.* NY: Oxford University Press.

Teacher Created Resources Staff (1999). *The best of multiple intelligences activities.* Westminster, CA: Teacher Created Materials.

Thimmesh, C. (2000). *Girls think of everything: Stories of ingenious inventions by women.* Boston: Houghton Mifflin.

Tucker, T. & Loehle, R. (1995). *Brainstorm! The stories of twenty American kid inventors*. NY: Farrar Straus & Giroux.

Tyre, P. (2006, January 30th). The trouble with boys. *Newsweek*, 44-52.

United States Patent and Trademark Office. (1990). *Buttons to biotech (1996 update report with supplemental data through 1998): Patenting by women, 1977 - 1988.* http://www.uspto.gov/web/offices/ac/ido/oeip/taf/wom_98.pdf

Waters, R. (2004, November 14). The Baby Brain Connection: Armed with new research on developing brain structure, social workers can help fix troubled baby/parent relationships. *The San Francisco Chronicle*. Sunday paper. http://www.sfgate.com/health/article/The-Baby-Brain-Connection-Armed-with-new-2672397.php

Watson, C. M., Quatman, T., & Elder, E. (2002). Career aspirations of adolescent girls: effects of achievement level, grade, and single-sex school environment. *Sex Roles: A Journal of Research, 46*(9-10), 323-335.

Weber, R. J. (1992). *Forks, phonographs, and hot air balloons: A field guide to inventive thinking*. NY: Oxford University Press.

Weil, E. (2008, March 2nd). Teaching boys and girls separately. *The New York Times Magazine*.

Westberg, K. L. (1998, September). Stimulating Children's Creative Thinking with the Invention Process. *Parenting for High Potential*, 18-20, 25.

Wolfe, M. F. (2000). *Rube Goldberg: Inventions*. NY: Simon & Schuster.

Wuffson, D. L. (1997). *The Kid Who Invented the Popsicle and Other Inspiring Stories About Inventions*. NY: Cobblehill Books. Zhensun, Z. & Low, A. (1991). *A Young Painter: The Life and Paintings of Wang Yani—China's Extraordinary Young Artist*. NY: Scholastic.